# 103 Great Poems

## 103 Meistergedichte

# Johann Wolfgang von Goethe

*A Dual-Language Book*

Edited and Translated by
STANLEY APPELBAUM

## DOVER PUBLICATIONS, INC.
Mineola, New York

## Bibliographical Note

This Dover edition, first published in 1999, reprints the complete text of 103 poems from a standard German text. The selection was made by Stanley Appelbaum, who also provided new English translations, an Introduction and Commentary, and other apparatus (see Contents for details).

### Library of Congress Cataloging-in-Publication Data

Goethe, Johann Wolfgang von, 1749–1832.
  [Poems. English & German. Selections]
  103 great poems : a dual-language book = 103 Meistergedichte / Johann Wolfgang von Goethe ; edited and translated by Stanley Appelbaum.
      p.     cm.
  ISBN 0-486-40667-9
  1. Goethe, Johann Wolfgang von, 1749–1832—Translations in English. I. Appelbaum, Stanley. II. Title. III. Title: One hundred three great poems. IV. Title: 103 Meistergedichte.
  PT2026.A3A56    1999
  831'.6—dc21
                                                   98-49292
                                                    CIP

Manufactured in the United States of America
Dover Publications, Inc., 31 East 2nd Street, Mineola, N.Y. 11501

# Contents

Contents v

# Introduction and Commentary

## I. Goethe's Life and Poetry

Johann Wolfgang Goethe, generally considered Germany's greatest literary figure, enjoyed such a long and productive life that, for the present purposes, only the barest outline must suffice. He was born in Frankfurt am Main in 1749. His paternal grandfather had made so much money as a master tailor and hotelkeeper that his son, the poet's father, could get along doing nothing in particular, and the poet, though ashamed of the source of his comforts, never suffered any privations in childhood and youth (after which he had his Weimar salary to live on).

Wolfgang wrote verse as a young boy, and continued to compose poems in the light, amorous style of the day ("Anacreontic style") while studying law in Leipzig from 1765 to 1768. It was only while completing his studies in Strasbourg in 1770–71 that he began speaking with a personal voice and breaking new ground in his poetry. This phenomenon is associated both with the influence of the literary historian Johann Gottfried Herder and with Goethe's love for a local parson's daughter, Friederike Brion, the first of his world-famous affairs. He now turned his hand to ballads and poetry in a folk vein, among other genres.

Goethe's law practice never amounted to much, but his literary reputation began to grow. In 1772 he began his series of "great hymns" in free verse, and soon found himself the chief spokesman for the "Sturm und Drang" (Storm and Stress) movement of rebellious young antiestablishment "geniuses." In 1774 he achieved instant and lasting fame with his novel *Die Leiden des jungen Werthers* (The Sorrows of Young Werther) and his boisterous historical drama *Götz von Berlichingen*.

The decisive turning point in the poet's life came in 1775, when the young Duke of Weimar, one of the dozens of independent sovereigns of the Germany of that time, invited Goethe to his court, where the poet was to remain (except for his two-year Italian escapade in 1786–88) for the remainder of his days, at first as a statesman-of-all-use; after Italy, chiefly as a sort of "minister of culture." The first version of (Part One of) *Faust*, the so-called *Urfaust*, was complete before the actual move to Weimar.

That important year, 1775, had also seen Goethe's attachment and brief engagement to another important inspirer of poems, Lili Schönemann.

During Goethe's first eleven years in Weimar, up to 1786, he wrote: the first draft of the novel *Wilhelm Meisters Lehrjahre* (Wilhelm Meister's Years of Apprenticeship), with its famous Mignon and Harpist poems; many poems inspired by his love for the lady-in-waiting Charlotte von Stein; and his play *Egmont*. In these years of maturing and of public responsibilities, he increasingly turned away from an attitude of rebellion to one of settled wisdom and enthusiasm for the "classical" achievements of the ancient Greeks and Romans. Largely in connection with mineral prospecting for the duke, he also formed his lifelong interest in natural history and scientific questions. In 1782 Goethe was created a nobleman, Johann Wolfgang *von* Goethe.

Aching for greater independence, and eager to see whether his talent for sketching really promised a career as a painter, in 1786 Goethe escaped to Italy without taking formal leave. He remained there, chiefly in Rome, for two years, happier, perhaps, than ever before. On his return in 1788 (the duke, who genuinely liked him, bore no grudge), Goethe began writing his famous *Römische Elegien* and began his liaison with Christiane Vulpius, whom he eventually married in 1806, touched by her brave defense of their home against French invaders after Napoleon's victory at Jena (she died in 1816). The late 1780s also saw the composition of Goethe's two greatest verse plays, *Iphigenie auf Tauris* and *Torquato Tasso*.

The 1790s were characterized for Goethe chiefly by his fruitful association ("friendship" is too strong a word) with the poet, playwright, historian, and literary theorist Friedrich Schiller; direct participation, as an observer, in battles against revolutionary France; the definitive version of *Wilhelm Meisters Lehrjahre*; the great "year of ballads," 1797; and the resumption of work on Part One of *Faust,* eventually published in 1808.

The last thirty years of the poet's life need not be recounted in detail. More and more he was the elder statesman, the guardian of tradition (somewhat unjust to newer talents in all the arts); a visit to his Weimar home, already a museum, was *de rigueur* for every cultured traveler to Germany; his pontificating "conversations" were duly recorded for publication; his correspondence with scholars and well-wishers was truly international. But he also continued to write novels, stories, and great poetry, both independent lyric poems and material that would ultimately be included in Part Two of *Faust* (published posthumously in 1833). And great surprises were still in store.

In 1814–15 Goethe's romance with Marianne von Willemer produced one of the most remarkable books of verse of all time, the *West-östlicher*

*Divan* (Occidental-Oriental Divan), amazingly bold, vigorous, fresh, and beautiful for a sexagenarian. And then the final great love, for Ulrike von Levetzow, 1821–23, found immortality in the Marienbad *Elegie.*

Mentally active to the last, Goethe died at eighty-two in 1832. (Further biographical details, as they specifically illuminate the poems in this anthology, will be found in the Commentary.)

※

Goethe wrote a vast amount: poems, novels, stories, plays both in prose and in verse, an autobiography, travel accounts, reminiscences of specific experiences, and scientific treatises, not to mention the journals, the voluminous correspondence, and the extensive recorded conversations. His poetic gift was the constant, unfailing element throughout this long and varied career; for his whole life, lyric verse was the chosen vessel into which he poured his soul-searching, his yearning for experimentation, and his wide-ranging speculation. Today the lyric poetry and *Faust* are seen as probably his most valuable legacy. His novels were crucial to the development of the form in Germany, but are not really of the same "world class" as those of, say, Cervantes and Tolstoy. His plays, though full of beauties, are not nearly as stageworthy as Schiller's. His scientific writings, of which he was so proud, and which claimed so much of his time, are just about totally superseded: without mathematical grounding, he literally attempted to be a Renaissance man in a period already characterized by specialized research; and scientific objectivity was altogether alien to his nature.

But the corpus of lyric poems, ballads, and elegies is possibly unique in world literature in extent, scope, and value, one of the most priceless possessions of German speakers, and worthy of close attention by all other lovers of literature. If an understanding of the basic meaning of a poem on its merely verbal level can be an aid to a deeper understanding—and it surely can—the present volume, with its representative selection of good, great, and very great Goethe poems, may play its humble part.

## II. The Nature of This Anthology

This volume contains a new selection of 103 poems, each absolutely complete, ranging over Goethe's entire career. The earliest included was written when he was eighteen; the latest, when he was eighty. Only a very few of the (relatively trivial) pre-1771 poems are given as a sampling of promising juvenilia; on the other hand, his late work, now appreciated more than ever, is generously represented. Here will be found many, if

not most, of the lyric poems on which his reputation is based; and readers acquainted with famous Goethe quotations will find their sources and contexts here in numerous instances. The selection includes great variety and many contrasts in mood, technique, and style. There are very long and very short lyrics; poems festive, philosophical, carefree, contemplative, narrative, didactic; and some of the world's greatest love poetry.

In two respects, sequence and criteria for inclusion, one very special edition of the complete poems has been followed here: *Goethes Gedichte in zeitlicher Folge* (Goethe's Poems in Chronological Order), first published by the Insel Verlag in 1916 and often reprinted since. With regard to sequence: this Dover edition does not deviate from that chronological sequence, even though the dates of some poems are in dispute (most poems are securely dated by journal entries, mentions in letters, or attendant circumstances); the Commentary, section III of this Introduction, discusses problematic dates.

With regard to inclusion: this volume uses the same standards as the chronological German edition. Poems from the *West-östlicher Divan* are included, although that cycle is normally printed separately from the *Gedichte* in complete-works editions. Poems embedded in other works— such as *Faust*, the novel *Wilhelm Meisters Lehrjahre*, the story *Novelle*, and various minor stage works—are included here if Goethe himself (or, occasionally, a later editor) included them in the *Gedichte*. No new excerpting has been done! Thus, from *Faust*, only "Der König in Thule" will be found here. There are no excerpts from such verse plays as *Iphigenie auf Tauris* or *Torquato Tasso*, no excerpts from such epic poems as *Hermann und Dorothea* or other nonlyric poetic productions.

The poems are printed here in their final, definitive forms, even though the dating used for their sequence is that of the earliest version. (In later life, Goethe did not do much rewriting, but, when preparing the 1789 edition of his works, he revised many of his poems of the 1760s and 1770s extensively—usually for the better, though a critic will now and then complain of a "loss of freshness.") It is impossible in a volume of this introductory nature to tabulate the successive versions of a poem. Also intentionally disregarded here is the sometimes very complicated publication history of the poems (many were not published until decades after they were written, some not at all in Goethe's lifetime).

The dates given are always those of composition, unless otherwise stated. Although every statistic is welcome to a true Goethe enthusiast, the Commentary only occasionally refers to the place where a given poem was written; on the other hand, more is said about the women who inspired certain poems. There are various textual traditions in Goethe

scholarship, and so, even though this volume contains "final" texts, the alert reader may still find small discrepancies between this text and other editions in such matters as punctuation (which Goethe himself never troubled with), word forms, and, in one or two places, even word choices. Since most readers are likely to have access to Goethe's lyrics, ballads, and elegies (aside from anthologies) in the *Gedichte* section of complete-works editions, the Commentary section of this Introduction indicates for each appropriate poem the subdivision of the *Gedichte* into which Goethe himself placed it in the last edition (1827) that he personally supervised (known in German as the *Ausgabe letzter Hand*). Some of these placements strike us as strange; poems of exactly the same nature or origin are put into widely separated subdivisions. In doing so, Goethe was sometimes deliberately throwing people off the track with regard to the women he was addressing, and sometimes he was filling out emptier sections or yielding to some other such publishing exigency; nevertheless, there is some degree of arbitrariness.

The 1827 subdivisions are as follows: "I. Lieder" (Songs). "II. Gesellige Lieder" (Convivial Songs). "III. Balladen" (Ballads). "IV. Elegien" (Elegies). "V. Episteln" (Epistles). "VI. Epigramme" (Epigrams). "VII. Weissagungen des Bakis" (Predictions of Bakis). "VIII. Vier Jahreszeiten" (Four Seasons). "IX. Sonette" (Sonnets). "X. Kantaten" (Cantatas). "XI. Vermischte Gedichte" (Miscellaneous Poems). "XII. Aus Wilhelm Meister" (From *Wilhelm Meister*). "XIII. Antiker Form sich nähernd" (Imitative of Greco-Roman Meters). "XIV. An Personen" (To Individuals). "XV. Kunst" (Art). "XVI. Parabolisch" (Parables). "XVII. Gott, Gemüt und Welt" (God, Mind, and World). "XVIII. Sprichwörtlich" (Proverbs). "XIX. Epigrammatisch" (Epigrams). "XX. Lyrisches" (Lyrics). "XXI. Loge" (Masonic). "XXII. Gott und Welt" (God and World). "XXIII. Aus Fremden Sprachen" (Translations). "XXIV. Zahme Xenien" (Tame Xenia [Gifts to Guests]). "XXV. Inschriften, Denk- und Sende-Blätter" (Inscriptions and Commemorative Poems).

This anthology has drawn only from subdivisions I, II, III, IV, XI, XII, XIII, XV, XX, and XXII. The vast amount of epigrams, polemics, occasional verse, album entries, poems to individuals on subjects of immediate interest, and the like, has been purposely omitted here (invaluable though it is to Goethe specialists) because of the ensuing necessity for endless, boring annotation and because of the relative lack of poetic merit. Only poems of manifestly universal interest and verbal beauty have been included, not poems that are chiefly of importance to German cultural history specifically. (Nevertheless, the serious student of Goethe cannot afford to overlook the rest if pursuing further study.)

This translation, in prose, following the German line for line to the extent that the differences between the languages allow, is meant to be as complete and accurate as possible, while conveying the mood and tone of the original in each case; often, in very idiomatic situations, the translation has had to be "idea for idea" rather than word for word, but no idea has been omitted or gratuitously introduced. The intention throughout was to provide the actual meaning of the German text (or at least one acceptable meaning; some of these "polyvalent" texts have caused experts to disagree on interpretation and even on their syntax!); this literal meaning can serve as a basis for appreciation of the intense beauty of the poems and the other qualities that elevate them to the highest literary plane.

Much attention has been paid to the special difficulties inherent in understanding Goethe's poetry. Not only has there been a fair amount of semantic change since his day; in addition, any interpretation must take into account his bold coinage of new words and compounds; such personal practices as the use of simple verbs in meanings they usually have only when a specific prefix is added (e.g., *eignen* for *aneignen* in the next-to-last line of the poem "Siebenschläfer"); and the specific connotations given to many words connected with the poet's scientific or philosophical ideas (often, only a knowledge of other writings of his can provide the key). The task of the present translator would have been considerably more difficult, if not impossible, without the commentary in *Goethe •*
*Gedichte / Herausgegeben und kommentiert von Erich Trunz* (C. H. Beck, Munich, 1981) and the specialized dictionary *Goethe-Wortschatz,* by Paul Fischer (Emil Rohmkopf, Leipzig, 1921)—though many other works were consulted.

The Commentary that follows treats each poem individually, though it indicates various formal and informal groupings. It supplies the dates of original composition and the subdivision of the *Gedichte* (or *West-östlicher Divan*) in which each poem is located. In addition, there is information on addressees, on Goethe's original intentions for the poems (inclusion in a play, commissioned festival piece, etc.), the places of the poems within his œuvre, special metrical or stanza forms, and all sorts of background information (references to mythology, current events, etc.). No footnotes have been placed on the text pages; all explanatory material is in the Commentary.

## III. Commentary on the Individual Poems

In this Commentary (but nowhere else in the volume) the poems selected are numbered from 1 to 103 for convenience and conciseness in cross-

referencing. The dates given are those of first composition (the basis for the sequence adopted here). The information beginning "In 1827 ed.:" indicates the specific subdivision of the section *Gedichte* in which Goethe placed the poem in question in the complete-works edition of 1827, the last one he personally supervised (the 1827 arrangement is the basis of almost all later editions of the complete poems).

1. "An den Schlaf." 1767. Not in 1827 ed. Goethe wrote this while a law student in Leipzig and included it in a small manuscript collection he called *Annette,* probably named for Anna Katharina Schönkopf, one of his Leipzig flames.

2. "Die schöne Nacht." 1768. In 1827 ed.: "I. Lieder." First title: "Die Nacht." Luna is the moon; Zephyr, the west wind.

3. "Am Flusse." Ca. 1768–69. In 1827 ed.: "I. Lieder." In 1798 Goethe sent the manuscript to Schiller for publication in one of his literary yearbooks, saying it was about thirty years old and the earliest piece he had available.

4. "Willkommen und Abschied." 1771. In 1827 ed.: "I. Lieder." Poems 4–6 were all addressed to Friederike Brion, a pastor's daughter in a village near Strasbourg, where Goethe was working toward his law degree. This group of poems marks the first major turning point in the poet's literary career; he was now speaking with his own voice, breaking new ground, and beginning to act as the spokesman for his generation.

5. "Mit einem gemalten Band." 1771. In 1827 ed.: "I. Lieder." Another Friederike poem (see No. 4). Hand-painted ribbons were frequently given as gifts to girlfriends. Zephyr: see No. 2.

6. "Mailied." 1771. In 1827 ed.: "I. Lieder." Another Friederike poem (see No. 4). First title: "Maifest." This has been called Goethe's best poem up to that time.

7. "Heidenröslein." 1771. In 1827 ed.: "I. Lieder." First title: "Fabelliedchen." This was Goethe's first important poem in folk-song style. Johann Gottfried Herder introduced him to the genre in Strasbourg. There is a specific flower called *Heiderose,* equivalent to sun rose or rock rose (*Cistus* and *Helianthemum* spp.).

8. "Wanderers Sturmlied." 1772. In 1827 ed.: "XI. Vermischte Gedichte." This was the first of Goethe's "great hymns" of the "Sturm und Drang" period (Storm and Stress; named for a 1776 play by Friedrich Maximilian von Klinger; for other "hymns" in the group, see Nos. 10, 14, 15, and 16). The "Sturm und Drang" movement, led by Goethe, was a youthful, hotheaded reaction against the generally placid and playful literature prevailing at the time (late Baroque and Rococo). The *Wanderer*

in Goethe's poems usually refers to himself; a great hiker, he had earned that nickname in real life. The term *Genius*, here interpretively translated as "inborn ability" (its special connotation in this poem), is based on the ancient Roman belief in a personal guardian spirit born along with the individual; the "Sturm und Drang" writers were sarcastically called "geniuses" by their opponents, and the period is often referred to as the *Geniezeit*. Deucalion's flood, in Greek mythology, was roughly the equivalent of Noah's in the Bible. Apollo gained the title Pythius after slaying the dragon Pytho near Delphi. The "son of water and earth" is mud. Bromius is a title of Dionysus, god of wine. The ancient Greek poet Pindar, composer of odes honoring victors in athletic games, was the chief inspiration for this kind of poem by Goethe; at the time it was still incorrectly thought that Pindar had written in free, untrammeled, short lines like Goethe's here. Phoebus Apollo is the sun; the evergreen cedar does not have to await the sun's springtime strength in order to be green. Jupiter Pluvius is the god of rain. The Castalian spring on Mount Parnassus was cited as the source of literary inspiration. Pindar, the poem says, will now be Goethe's model instead of the gentle love lyricist Anacreon or the writer of bucolic idylls Theocritus (all ancient Greek poets; for Anacreon, see also No. 40). Sybaris was a Greek town in southern Italy.

9. "Zigeunerlied." 1771. In 1827 ed.: "II. Gesellige Lieder." Inserted at the opening of Act Five of the first version of Goethe's play *Götz von Berlichingen*, where one of the female characters, riding through a forest to rejoin her husband, gets lost and falls in with the Gypsy women who sing the song. In the play, the first four lines of each stanza are performed by one old woman; the next two lines, imitating the wolves' howling (*wau wau* = bowwow), by the whole group; and the last line, imitating the owls' calls (*wito hu* = to-whoo), by a different soloist. This is an early example of Goethe's affinity for the macabre and uncanny.

10. "Mahomets Gesang." 1772–73. In 1827 ed.: "XI. Vermischte Gedichte." Another of the "great hymns" of the "Sturm und Drang" (see No. 8), this was originally intended to be spoken by Mohammed's daughter Fatima and her husband Ali in the unfinished play *Mahomet*. The poem, which refers to the Prophet's meteoric career, anthropomorphizes the river (the *er* in German is, naturally, much less obtrusive than the "he" that a translator is almost compelled to use). The "cedar houses" are, of course, ships.

11. "Das Veilchen." 1773–74. In 1827 ed.: "III. Balladen." Goethe inserted this poem into his Singspiel (play with songs) *Erwin und Elmire*, in which Elmire, who has driven away Erwin by her indifference, recalls

it as a song that Erwin used to serenade her with. She performs it with two of her friends, a man and a woman.

12. "Der untreue Knabe." Ca. 1774. In 1827 ed.: "III. Balladen." The abrupt ending is intentional. Goethe inserted this poem into a Singspiel called *Claudine von Villa Bella*, where it is sung by a high-minded bandit chieftain who is visiting a noble home in disguise; his performance is interrupted by the arrival of other characters bringing important news.

13. "Der König in Thule." 1774. In 1827 ed.: "III. Balladen." This song, sung by Margarete (Gretchen) in the First Part of *Faust* as she is undressing just before she finds the casket of jewels Faust has left for her, already appeared in the same position in the early version of the play known as the *Urfaust* (completed by 1775). In Greco-Roman geography, Thule was a country in the northwestern corner of the world (perhaps Iceland).

14. "Ganymed." 1774. In 1827 ed.: "XI. Vermischte Gedichte." Another of the "great hymns" of the "Sturm und Drang" period (see No. 8). Ganymede was a handsome Trojan boy abducted by Zeus's eagle; on Olympus, Ganymede served as a cupbearer to the gods and a lover of Zeus. The "your" in the fifth line from the end is plural and refers to the clouds.

15. "An Schwager Kronos." 1774. In 1827 ed.: "XI Vermischte Gedichte." Another "great hymn" (see No. 8). As so frequently, Kronos (the father of Zeus and other Olympians) is here confused with Chronos (time), who is really intended. Orcus is another name for Hades, or hell.

16. "Prometheus." 1774. In 1827 ed.: "XI. Vermischte Gedichte." Another "great hymn" (see No. 8). Originally a speech by Prometheus in an unfinished play.

17. "Neue Liebe neues Leben." 1775. In 1827 ed.: "I. Lieder." One of the poems (the first?) written during Goethe's brief romance and engagement with Lili (Anna Elizabeth) Schönemann, daughter of a Frankfurt banker.

18. "Auf dem See." 1775. In 1827 ed.: "I. Lieder." The lake is the Lake of Zurich; the poem was written on an outing to Switzerland. The unusual opening—the "Und" is like a deep breath preliminary to a vigorous oar stroke—is due to one of the many felicitous revisions of earlier poems that Goethe undertook for a 1789 edition; the original wording was truly grotesque.

19. "Bundeslied." 1775. In 1827 ed.: "II. Gesellige Lieder." This "eternal" alliance was very small and very brief. The poem was written to celebrate a wedding that Goethe and Lili attended.

20. "Wonne der Wehmut." 1775. In 1827 ed.: "I. Lieder."

21. "Jägers Abendlied." Winter 1775–76. In 1827 ed.: "I. Lieder."

Written very early in Goethe's Weimar sojourn, this poem has been seen by some as a reminiscence of Lili, by others as a homage to the new Weimar love, Charlotte von Stein.

22. "Hoffnung." 1776. In 1827 ed.: "I. Lieder."

23. "Wandrers Nachtlied." 1776. In 1827 ed.: "I. Lieder." On Goethe as *Wanderer,* see comments on No. 8.

24. "An Charlotte von Stein." 1776, in a letter to her. Not in 1827 edition. On his arrival in Weimar, Goethe, like many "geniuses" of the "Sturm und Drang," was still to some extent uncouth and a roughneck. Frau von Stein, a lady-in-waiting at the ducal court, took him in hand and smoothed away the rough edges, readying him for court life. Eventually Goethe addressed some 1,700 letters to her.

25. "Rastlose Liebe." 1776. In 1827 ed.: "I. Lieder." Written during a mission for the Weimar court. *Rastlos* can also be translated as "incessant" or "tireless."

26. "Alles geben die Götter, die unendlichen." 1777, in a letter to Countess Auguste Stolberg, with whom Goethe corresponded until 1823 without ever meeting her in person (she was the sister of close friends). Not in 1827 edition. The letter containing the poem also mentions the death of Goethe's sister Cornelia, of whom he was intensely fond. Other editions give the first words as "Alles geben Götter" or "Alles gaben Götter."

27. "An den Mond." 1778. In 1827 ed.: "I. Lieder." Goethe's definitive version. This poem was addressed to Frau von Stein, who wrote a parody of it after Goethe left her.

28. "Harzreise im Winter." Winter 1777–78, written immediately after the journey to the Harz mountain range. In 1827 ed.: "XI. Vermischte Gedichte." Goethe's own commentary is helpful, because the difficulty of the poem lies in the omission of background data, that is, in the poet's symbolic selection of disparate parts of his actual experiences on the journey. The Harz mountains lay within the territories belonging to the Duchy of Weimar, and Goethe was sent there to investigate the possibility of mining silver; he had the secondary, personal purpose of visiting a correspondent who was very downcast. Meanwhile, the duke and other courtiers were hunting wild boars. The poet is protected from all ills by his love (for Frau von Stein). Individual remarks: It was believed that certain birds, such as reed warblers (*Rohrsperlinge*) wintered in swamps. The "dreaded peak" is that of the Brocken, the highest summit in the Harz range and the legendary site of the witches' sabbath on Walpurgisnacht (the eve of May Day). The peak is said to have an "unexplored

bosom" because it had not been prospected for mining, though the veins (of metal) of its "brothers" had been.

29. "Der Fischer." 1778. In 1827 ed.: "III. Balladen." Possibly inspired by a recent suicide by drowning.

30. "Grenzen der Menschheit." Between 1778 and 1781. In 1827 ed.: "XI. Vermischte Gedichte." Although similar in form to "Prometheus" (No. 16), and intended as a pendant to it, this poem differs vastly in its philosophy, relegating man from supremacy to subordinacy, and preaching reserve and modesty. It can be seen as a portal to Goethe's Classical period, which corresponded in time to his increasing interest in Greco-Roman ideals and his settling into his position as a leading statesman.

31. "Gesang der Geister über den Wassern." 1779. In 1827 ed.: "XI. Vermischte Gedichte." Inspired by the sight of the Staubbach falls at Lauterbrunnen, Switzerland, the poem was conceived as a chant for two voices in alternation.

32. "Liebhaber in allen Gestalten." Before 1786; the chronological edition puts it in a 1779 or 1780 position. In 1827 ed.: "I. Lieder."

33. "Wandrers Nachtlied [Ein gleiches]." 1780. In 1827 ed.: "I. Lieder." Called "Ein gleiches" in complete-works editions, where it appears immediately after the first "Wandrers Nachtlied" (No. 23). Goethe wrote this on the wall of a wooden hut. Later this odd "manuscript" was protected by glass, and Goethe was able to revisit and authenticate it fifty-one years after writing it.

34. "Erlkönig." 1782. In 1827 ed.: "III. Balladen." Goethe included this ballad in his Singspiel Die Fischerin. Erlkönig literally is "alder king," but the Erl- is based on a mistaken eighteenth-century translation from a Danish source; the meaning is clearly "elf king."

35. "Der Sänger." 1783. In 1827 ed.: "III. Balladen." This poem was included in the first draft of a novel that Goethe worked on in the early 1780s; this first draft, which he never published, was called Wilhelm Meisters theatralische Sendung (Wilhelm Meister's Theatrical Vocation). In the 1790s Goethe revised it heavily, eventually publishing it as Wilhelm Meisters Lehrjahre (Wilhelm Meister's Years of Apprenticeship); he retained poems from the first draft, such as this one, and added new ones. This song is performed in the novel by a mysterious, melancholy itinerant harpist. For other Wilhelm Meister poems, see Nos. 36, 38, 41, 54, 55, and 58.

36. "Harfenspieler" ["Wer nie . . ."]. 1783. In 1827 ed.: "XII. Aus Wilhelm Meister." Another poem included in both the Theatralische Sendung and the Lehrjahre (see No. 35). In the poems with headings

"Harfenspieler" and "Mignon," those headings are not titles but indications of the respective speakers.

37. "Das Göttliche." 1783. In 1827 ed.: "XI. Vermischte Gedichte." A famous example of Goethe's new "Classical" ideals.

38. "Mignon" ["Kennst du . . ."]. 1784. In 1827 ed.: "III. Balladen." In both versions of *Wilhelm Meister* named in the comments on No. 35 (see also comments on No. 36). Mignon is an odd, sad waif hopelessly in love with Wilhelm.

39. "Zueignung." 1784. Originally written as an introduction to the uncompleted epic poem "Die Geheimnisse" (The Mysteries); in the 1827 edition, placed in the first volume at the head of Goethe's complete works. The stanzas are in *ottava rima* (iambic pentameter with rhyme scheme ABABABCC).

40. "Anakreons Grab." 1784–85. In 1827 ed.: "XIII. Antiker Form sich nähernd." In this, his Classical period, Goethe not only treated Greco-Roman subjects (Anacreon was a Greek poet of the sixth century B.C.), but also began imitating Greco-Roman meters. This poem is written in elegiac couplets (the "elegiac" has no connotation of sadness!), a dactylic hexameter followed by a dactylic pentameter:

$$—\cup\cup|—\cup\cup|—\cup\cup|—\cup\cup|—\cup\cup|—\ —$$
$$—\cup\cup|—\cup\cup|—|\,|—\cup\cup|—\cup\cup|—$$

Every dactyl (—∪∪), except the last one in each line, can be replaced by a spondee (— —). The last syllable in the hexameter lines can be short. Perfectly natural in languages such as ancient Greek and Latin, which had inherently long vowels and syllables, this meter is always strained in modern word-stress languages such as English and German; the reader must become a willing accomplice, first divining the poet's metrical intentions and then consciously placing the stresses in the "right" spots, even though different stresses may be possible—and even more congenial to the language!

41. "Mignon" ["Nur wer . . ."]. 1785. In 1827 ed.: "XII. Aus Wilhelm Meister." In *Wilhelm Meisters theatralische Sendung* (see No. 35) Mignon sings this by herself; in the *Lehrjahre* it is characterized as an irregular duo for her and the harpist. Tchaikovsky's song (known in English as "None but the Lonely Heart") is perhaps the best-known setting worldwide of any Goethe poem.

42. "Cophtisches Lied." 1787. In 1827 ed.: "II. Gesellige Lieder." This song and the next were written for the verse play *Die Mystifizierten,* which Goethe rewrote in prose as *Der Groß-Cophta* (completed 1791),

leaving out these poems. The "Great Cophta," a charlatan based on the real-life Cagliostro, is head of a Masonic-type lodge and involved in a scheme based on the real-life necklace affair of 1785 in which Marie-Antoinette was duped.

43. "Ein andres" [Cophtisches Lied II]. See comments on No. 42.

44. "Amor als Landschaftsmaler." 1787. In 1827 ed.: "XV. Kunst." Written during Goethe's stay in Italy, where he spent much of his time painting.

45–49. "Römische Elegien." In 1827 ed.: "IV. Elegien." This cycle of twenty poems, written in elegiac couplets (see comments on No. 40), was composed between 1788 and 1790, after Goethe's return to Weimar from his two-year Italian escapade. It was very soon after his return that he began living with Christiane Vulpius, whom he married many years later; this new love inspired the poetic cycle, which also contains reminiscences of Italian romances. In No. 46: The Trojan prince Anchises was a lover of Aphrodite, who gave birth to his son Aeneas. The sleeper loved by the moon goddess was Endymion. Aurora (Eos), goddess of dawn, had numerous human lovers. Leander drowned while swimming across the Hellespont for a tryst with Hero. The sons of Mars and Rhea Sylvia were Romulus and Remus, legendary founders of Rome. In No. 47: The rolling wheel was the punishment in Hades of the sinner Ixion; the punishment on the crag may refer either to Prometheus' enchainment in the Caucasus range or Sisyphus' fate of eternally pushing a rock uphill. Proteus and Thetis were marine deities who could change shape at will. In No. 48: Cupid's triumvirs are the three Roman elegiac poets Catullus, Tibullus, and Propertius.

50. "Der Rattenfänger." Ca. 1802? The chronological edition, followed here for sequence, places it in the late 1780s or early 1790s. In 1827 ed.: "III. Balladen." Possibly written for a children's ballet.

51. "Die Spinnerin." 1795? In 1827 ed.: "III. Balladen." Strictly speaking, *Stein* is one fifth of a metric hundredweight.

52 & 53. "Meeres Stille" & "Glückliche Fahrt." 1795 or earlier. In 1827 ed.: "I. Lieder." A diptych. Aeolus is the god of the winds.

54. "Mignon" ["Heiß mich . . ."]. 1795? At least two authoritative references assign the poem to that year; however, it is included, in an appropriate narrative context, in at least one modern edition of the *Theatralische Sendung* (see No. 35), which is supposed to have been completed in 1785. Included in the *Lehrjahre*. In 1827 ed.: "XII. Aus Wilhelm Meister." In both versions of the novel, Mignon is here reciting from a role in a play (which nevertheless suits her own situation).

55. "Harfenspieler" ["An die Türen . . ."]. 1795? In 1827 ed.: "XII. Aus

Wilhelm Meister." Not in the *Sendung* (see No. 35). In the *Lehrjahre,* this is characterized as the final stanza of a song consoling one who is close to madness.

56. "Nähe des Geliebten." 1795. In 1827 ed.: "I. Lieder." A rewriting by Goethe of a poem by the poetess Friederike Brun, in which he saw possibilities, if improved.

57. "Wer kauft Liebesgötter?" 1795. In 1827 ed.: "I. Lieder." From a sequel to *Die Zauberflöte* (The Magic Flute); in this scene Papageno and Papagena come in with cages containing winged children.

58. "Mignon" ["So laßt . . ."]. 1796. In 1827 ed.: "XII. Aus Wilhelm Meister." Not in *Sendung,* only in *Lehrjahre* (see No. 35). Near to death, Mignon here refuses to take off an angel's costume she has worn at a religious pageant.

59. "Der Schatzgräber." 1797. In 1827 ed.: "III. Balladen." Inspired by an illustration in an edition of Petrarch and the description of a magical rite in the autobiography of Cellini, which Goethe translated. In friendly rivalry, Goethe and Schiller wrote some of their greatest poems in ballad form during 1797, the *Balladenjahr.* (See also Nos. 60–62.)

60. "Die Braut von Korinth." 1797. In 1827 ed.: "III. Balladen." The gifts of Ceres and Bacchus are bread and wine, respectively. Hymen is the torch-bearing god of marriage. Salt and [holy] water: used at funerals.

61. "Der Gott und die Bajadere." 1797. In 1827 ed.: "III. Balladen." Bayadere: a dancer-prostitute in India; from the Portuguese *bailadeira,* "dancing girl." *Mahadöh:* Mahadev(a), "great god," a title of Shiva; Shiva is not known for incarnations (avatars), unlike the god Vishnu; at an early stage, Goethe called this poem "Ram und die Bajadere," and Ram(a) *is* one of the two most important avatars of Vishnu. The sixth line can also be rendered as: "allowing anything to happen to him." Bouquet: part of the dancing girl's reception ceremony.

62. "Der Zauberlehrling." 1797. In 1827 ed.: "III. Balladen." Made even more popular by Dukas's tone poem and Disney's use of the music in *Fantasia.* Based on a narrative by the ancient Greek satirist Lucian.

63. "Der Musensohn." 1799. In 1827 ed.: "I. Lieder."

64. ["Sonett."] 1802. Not in 1827 edition. Originally part of the prologue for the opening of a Weimar ducal theater in the town of Bad Lauchstädt.

65. "Tischlied." 1802. In 1827 ed.: "II. Gesellige Lieder." For a banquet at an exclusive social club that was attended by the Duke of Weimar and his son.

66. "Schäfers Klagelied." 1802. In 1827 ed.: "I. Lieder." In folk-song style.

67. "Epilog zu Schillers Glocke." 1805–15. In 1827 ed.: "XI. Vermischte Gedichte." Spoken in 1805, shortly after Schiller's death, as an epilogue to a dramatization of Schiller's poem "Das Lied von der Glocke" (The Song of the Bell), in which the stages in the casting of a church bell are associated with the stages in a typical human life. Goethe's epilogue, written in *ottava rima* (see comments on No. 39), was later updated for anniversary performances of the same dramatization in 1810 and 1815. The "we" and "us" in the poem are said from the actors' viewpoint. The epigraph consists of the last two lines of Schiller's poem, which refer to the bell. When the son of the Duke of Weimar married a daughter of the Russian Czar in 1804 (the "young princely couple"), Schiller wrote a celebratory play called *Die Huldigung der Künste* (Homage of the Arts). Various stanzas in this "Epilogue" commemorate Schiller as an astronomer, historian, idealist, and playwright. Schiller suffered during all of his life from tuberculosis.

68. "Vanitas! vanitatum vanitas!" 1806. In 1827 ed.: "II. Gesellige Lieder." The title is a (Latin) quotation from Ecclesiastes. It was written as a parody of a religious poem.

69. "Metamorphose der Tiere." Usually dated 1806, but possibly written earlier (it has been considered to be a fragment of a long poem about nature—like the ancient Roman Lucretius's *De rerum natura*—that Goethe was working on in 1798–99). In 1827 ed.: "XXII. Gott und Welt." (Goethe also wrote a corresponding poem about plants.) Written in dactylic hexameter (see No. 40). An outstanding example of Goethe's didactic poetry.

70. "Schweizerlied." 1811, or possibly much earlier. In 1827 ed.: "II. Gesellige Lieder." A folk-song adaptation in a readily understandable Alamannic dialect; a poem of great charm and technical skill for all its simplicity.

71. "Der Totentanz." 1813. In 1827 ed.: "III. Balladen."

72. "Die wandelnde Glocke." 1813. In 1827 ed.: "III. Balladen." The German poem does not indicate the child's sex. To avoid calling a young human being "it," and because the freedom of behavior described may have been more likely to pertain to a male child at the time, male pronouns have been used in the translation. In some editions, in the fourth stanza, the punctuation comes after "Schrecken," and the new sentence begins with "Hinterher."

73. "Gefunden." 1813. In 1827 ed.: "I. Lieder." Written for the twenty-fifth anniversary of the beginning of Goethe's relationship with his wife Christiane.

74. "Ballade." 1813 (last two stanzas, 1816). In 1827 ed.: "XX. Lyrisches." Based on a Percy ballad and a *Decameron* story. Goethe wrote a commentary that adds no information, but merely retells the story for those unfamiliar with ballad narrative techniques.

75. "Kriegsglück." 1814. In 1827 ed.: "II. Gesellige Lieder." The German war of liberation from Napoleon's clutches elicited some of the greatest patriotic poems in the language—from others! Goethe was content with amusing trifles like this.

76–88 were not published until 1819, in the volume *West-östlicher Divan* (Occidental-Oriental Divan). "Divan" is a Persian term for a book of poetry all by one author; Goethe was specifically inspired by the poems of Hafiz (died ca. A.D. 1389). Goethe's romance with Marianne von Willemer, mistress, then wife, of a Frankfurt banker, was another major inspiration; the most talented of all Goethe's amours, Marianne actually wrote (uncredited) some of the poems in the *Divan*. In most editions of Goethe, the *Divan* is kept strictly separate from the *Gedichte*; thus, in the comments that follow, instead of the 1827 subdivisions of the *Gedichte*, the books into which the *Divan* is subdivided are indicated.

76. "Elemente." 1814. From "Moganni Nameh/Buch des Sängers" (Book of the Singer).

77. "Phänomen." 1814. From the Book of the Singer (see No. 76). Phoebus is the sun. Rainbows were of interest to Goethe in his studies of optics and color theory.

78. "Solang man nüchtern ist." 1814. From "Saki Nameh/Das Schenkenbuch" (Book of the Cupbearer). Although drunkenness, in Islamic Sufi literature, is a metaphor for religious rapture, Goethe actually was a copious drinker (but not an alcoholic!) all his life.

79. "Selige Sehnsucht." 1814. From the Book of the Singer (see No. 76).

80. "Schenke" ["Nennen dich . . ."]. 1814. From the Book of the Cupbearer (see No. 78). One of the traditional figures in classical Islamic poetry was the good-looking boy serving the poet as cupbearer; a homoerotic tinge was always present in such poems. The heading indicates the speaker.

81. "Siebenschläfer." 1814–15. From "Chuld Nameh/Buch des Paradieses" (Book of Paradise). Based on a well-known early Christian legend that was also adapted in the Koran. In Islam, Jesus is one of the great prophets. The persecuting emperor was Decius (reigned 248–251) and the sleep lasted about two hundred years.

82. "In tausend Formen magst du dich verstecken." 1815. From "Suleika Name/Buch Suleika" (Book of Suleika).

83. "Lied und Gebilde." 1815. From the Book of the Singer (see No. 76).

84 & 85. "Hatem" ["Nicht Gelegenheit . . ."] & "Suleika" ["Hochbe-glückt . . ."]. 1815. From the Book of Suleika (see No. 82). A pair of poems, statement and reply. No. 84 is said to be the first poem Goethe addressed to Marianne von Willemer. No. 85 was written by Marianne and revised by Goethe. The name Hatem was adopted from that of several Persian poets. Suleika is the Islamic name for the biblical Potiphar's wife, whose role is much more prominent and sympathetic in Islamic literature, where she appears as a great, sincere lover. In Goethe's "Hatem" and "Suleika" poems, the heading indicates the speaker.

86. "Als ich auf dem Euphrat schiffte." 1815. From the Book of Suleika (see No. 82). In some editions this is printed as two separate poems, and Hugo Wolf made two separate songs out of it. Suleika's part has been said to be Goethe's rewriting of Marianne's original. Each Ascension Day, the Doge of Venice symbolically married the sea by throwing a ring into it.

87. "Suleika" ["Was bedeutet . . ."]. 1815. From the Book of Suleika (see No. 82). Goethe's adaptation from Marianne. The "high walls" are those of the Heidelberg palace, where the couple met.

88. "Hatem" ["Locken, haltet . . ."]. 1815. From the Book of Suleika (see No. 82). The rhyme scheme indicates that, in the third stanza, "Hatem" is a substitution for "Goethe."

89. "Lust und Qual." 1815 or later. In 1827 ed.: "XX. Lyrisches."

90. "Prooemion." 1815–16. In 1827 ed.: "XXII. Gott und Welt." First published as the introductory poem to a new natural-history journal edited by Goethe.

91. "Urworte. Orphisch." 1817. In 1827 ed.: "XXII. Gott und Welt." Orphism was a mystical trend in ancient Greek religion, which its adherents traced back to the legendary bard Orpheus. Goethe, who was inspired by a passage in Macrobius (a Latin author of late antiquity), wrote his own commentary to this poem; but it only restates the same content in other words for the benefit of those totally incapable of reading poetry. The *daimon* (inborn guardian spirit) represents a person's basic nature and character; it is in itself unchangeable, but, as the subsequent stanzas show, chance, environment, love, and necessity also mold our fate, even to the point of negating free will. Hope remains to us.

92. "Eins und alles." 1821. In 1827 ed.: "XXII. Gott und Welt."

93. "Paria." 1821–23. In 1827 ed.: "XX. Lyrisches." A three-part poem sometimes spoken of as a trilogy. Based on a Hindu legend. Brahma is the creator god. The brahmans (priests), warriors (including rajahs), and

merchants are three of the chief traditional, generalized castes of Hinduism; pariahs are members of a very low caste who work at menial tasks and eat things not permitted to members of high castes. For the bayaderes and their goddess, see No. 61.

94–96. Originally written in this order as separate poems, these works were ultimately published by Goethe in the order 96-95-94 under the general title *Trilogie der Leidenschaft* (Trilogy of Passion), and appear as a trilogy in most editions.

94. "An Madame Marie Szymanowska" is the original title, changed to "Aussöhnung" for the trilogy. 1823. In 1827 ed.: "XX. Lyrisches" (the entire trilogy). Madame Szymanowska, a Pole, was a composer and a pianist at the Russian court. (She also was the mother-in-law of Adam Mickiewicz, one of the greatest Polish poets.) Goethe met her while taking the waters in Marienbad. Goethe was indeed fond of music, but his tastes ran to the light and bland. Of his great contemporaries, Beethoven totally disconcerted him, and he did not care much for Schubert or Weber. Goethe's own French translation of this poem, prepared for its addressee, whose German was poor, is relatively commonplace in diction, and shows all the more clearly, by contrast, just what a wizard he was with the German language.

95. "Elegie." 1823. Also known as the "Marienbad Elegy," this has been called Goethe's greatest poem. In this case, "elegy" definitely does connote melancholy. Goethe was mourning the failure of his relationship with the teenaged Ulrike von Levetzow in Marienbad; this had shattered him more than anything else in years, perhaps ever. The epigraph is a famous quotation from his own verse play *Torquato Tasso.* The "peace of God" is that mentioned by St. Paul in the *Epistle to the Philippians.* Pandora: in Greek mythology, a woman endowed with all gifts by the gods, but ultimately a disaster to mankind.

96. "An Werther." 1824. This was written for the fiftieth-anniversary edition (by the same publishers) of the novel *Die Leiden des jungen Werthers* (The Sorrows of Young Werther), which had made Goethe famous in 1774, while he was still an unknown lawyer. Werther commits suicide after a hopeless love affair. The last line of the poem is an echo of the lines from *Torquato Tasso* used in the epigraph to No. 95.

97. "Bei Betrachtung von Schillers Schädel." 1826. In 1827 ed.: "XI. Vermischte Gedichte." In 1826 Schiller's remains had to be reinterred, and Goethe kept the skull in his own home for a while. The poem is written in *terza rima* (iambic pentameter; rhyme scheme ABA BCB CDC . . .), like Dante's *Divine Comedy,* which Goethe was then reading in translation.

98. "Aus den Gruben, hier im Graben." 1826. Not in the *Gedichte* section of complete-works editions. This poem appears in the short story entitled simply *Novelle*, in which a mysterious boy rounds up a runaway lion with music and song. There is an overall allusion to the biblical story of Daniel in the lions' den. Goethe stated that he had first conceived the idea for the story in 1797.

99. "Dämmrung senkte sich von oben." 1827. From this point on, the poems were written too late to appear in the 1827 edition. This is No. VIII of a cycle of fourteen short lyrics called *Chinesich-Deutsche Jahres- und Tageszeiten* (Chinese-German Seasons and Times of Day), inspired by translations of Chinese stories and poems and by Chinese art. The miniature form, the capturing of a fleeting mood or thought, and the appreciation of nature comprise the chief Chinese elements. The term *Luna* for the moon is reminiscent of Goethe's earliest, Rococo poetry.

100. "Den Vereinigten Staaten." 1827. This is not a great poem, but the first line, at least, is a permanent part of German culture. The great days of German emigration to America were still in the future, but Goethe treated that theme in several works, including his *Wilhelm Meister* novels. Why the amusing reference to basalt? As an amateur geologist, Goethe sided vehemently with the Neptunist theory that all rocks were formed by the agency of water, and bitterly opposed the Vulcanists, or Plutonists, who credited igneous fusion with their origin; the nature of basalt was a powerful argument on the side of Goethe's opponents.

101. "Der Bräutigam." 1828. The last line is a variation of the very famous song of the lookout man Lynkeus in Act Five of the Second Part of *Faust:* "You fortunate eyes, / all that you ever saw, / however it may be, / it was so beautiful!"

102. "Dem aufgehenden Vollmonde." 1828. This poem is probably connected with a vow that Goethe and Marianne von Willemer made to think of each other whenever the full moon rose.

103. "Vermächtnis." 1829. Later editors placed this poem in section XXII ("Gott und Welt") of the *Gedichte*. It has been called Goethe's last great poem. Goethe told his memorialist Johann Peter Eckermann that it was a rebuttal to one of his own statements, the closing lines of "Eins und alles" (No. 92). The wise man who "taught" earth to circle the sun is Copernicus. This "legacy" is a fitting ending to the volume.

# 103 Great Poems

---

# 103 Meistergedichte

## An den Schlaf

Der du mit deinem Mohne
Selbst Götteraugen zwingst,
Und Bettler oft zum Throne,
Zum Mädchen Schäfer bringst,
Vernimm: Kein Traumgespinste
Verlang ich heut von dir,
Den größten deiner Dienste,
Geliebter, leiste mir.

An meines Mädchens Seite
Sitz ich, ihr Aug spricht Lust,
Und unter neidscher Seide
Steigt fühlbar ihre Brust;
Oft hatte meinen Küssen
Sie Amor zugebracht,
Dies Glück muß ich vermissen,
Die strenge Mutter wacht.

Am Abend triffst du wieder
Mich dort, o tritt herein,
Sprüh Mohn von dem Gefieder,
Da schlaf die Mutter ein:
Bei blassem Lichterscheinen
Von Lieb Annette warm
Sink, wie Mama in deinen,
In meinen giergen Arm.

## Die schöne Nacht

Nun verlaß ich diese Hütte,
Meiner Liebsten Aufenthalt,
Wandle mit verhülltem Schritte
Durch den öden finstern Wald.
Luna bricht durch Busch und Eichen,
Zephir meldet ihren Lauf,
Und die Birken streun mit Neigen
Ihr den süßten Weihrauch auf.

## *To Sleep*

You who with your poppy
have power even over the eyes of gods;
you who often bring beggars to the throne
and shepherds to their girls,
listen: no tissues of dream
do I demand of you today;
perform for me, dear one,
the greatest of your services.

By my girl's side
I sit; her eyes speak of pleasure,
and beneath the envious silk
her breast is heaving noticeably;
often in the past Cupid delivered her
to my kisses;
I now have to forgo that happiness,
her strict mother is on guard.

In the evening you will find
me there; oh, step in,
sprinkle poppy from your wings,
and send her mother to sleep:
by the pale light of the candles
let Annette, heated with love,
sink into my greedy arms
just as Mama sinks into yours.

## *The Beautiful Night*

Now I leave this cottage,
where my darling lives,
and walk with muffled steps
through the solitary, dark forest.
Luna breaks through bushes and oaks,
Zephyr announces her course,
and the birches, bowing, scatter
the sweetest incense before her.

Wie ergötz ich mich im Kühlen
Dieser schönen Sommernacht!
O wie still ist hier zu fühlen,
Was die Seele glücklich macht!
Läßt sich kaum die Wonne fassen!
Und doch wollt ich, Himmel, dir
Tausend solcher Nächte lassen,
Gäb mein Mädchen Eine mir.

## Am Flusse

Verfließet, vielgeliebte Lieder,
Zum Meere der Vergessenheit!
Kein Knabe sing entzückt euch wieder,
Kein Mädchen in der Blütenzeit.

Ihr sanget nur von meiner Lieben;
Nun spricht sie meiner Treue Hohn.
Ihr wart ins Wasser eingeschrieben,
So fließt denn auch mit ihm davon.

## Willkommen und Abschied

Es schlug mein Herz, geschwind zu Pferde!
Es war getan fast eh gedacht.
Der Abend wiegte schon die Erde,
Und an den Bergen hing die Nacht:
Schon stand im Nebelkleid die Eiche,
Ein aufgetürmter Riese, da,
Wo Finsternis aus dem Gesträuche
Mit hundert schwarzen Augen sah.

Der Mond von einem Wolkenhügel
Sah kläglich aus dem Duft hervor,
Die Winde schwangen leise Flügel,
Umsausten schauerlich mein Ohr;

How I delight in the coolness
of this beautiful summer night!
Oh, how calmly one can feel here
that which makes the soul happy!
The rapture can hardly be conceived!
And yet, heaven, I would
abandon a thousand such nights to you
if my girl gave me just one.

## By the River

Flow away, dearly beloved songs,
to the sea of forgetfulness!
Let no lad sing you again in delight,
no girl in the season of blossom.

You sang of my sweetheart only;
now she mocks my fidelity.
You were written on water,
and so flow away along with it.

## Welcome and Farewell

My heart beat: at once to horse!
The deed was nearly quicker than the thought.
Evening was already cradling the earth,
and night hung upon the mountains.
The oak already stood in its garment of mist,
a towering giant, there
where blackness peered from the bushes
with a hundred dark eyes.

From a hill of cloud the moon
looked lamentingly out of the haze;
the winds beat soft wings
and soughed fearfully around my ears;

Die Nacht schuf tausend Ungeheuer,
Doch frisch und fröhlich war mein Mut:
In meinen Adern welches Feuer!
In meinem Herzen welche Glut!

Dich sah ich, und die milde Freude
Floß von dem süßen Blick auf mich;
Ganz war mein Herz an deiner Seite
Und jeder Atemzug für dich.
Ein rosenfarbnes Frühlingswetter
Umgab das liebliche Gesicht,
Und Zärtlichkeit für mich – ihr Götter!
Ich hofft es, ich verdient es nicht!

Doch ach, schon mit der Morgensonne
Verengt der Abschied mir das Herz:
In deinen Küssen welche Wonne!
In deinem Auge welcher Schmerz!
Ich ging, du standst und sahst zur Erden,
Und sahst mir nach mit nassem Blick:
Und doch, welch Glück, geliebt zu werden!
Und lieben, Götter, welch ein Glück!

## Mit einem gemalten Band

Kleine Blumen, kleine Blätter
Streuen mir mit leichter Hand
Gute junge Frühlings-Götter
Tändelnd auf ein luftig Band.

Zephir, nimms auf deine Flügel,
Schlings um meiner Liebsten Kleid!
Und so tritt sie vor den Spiegel
All in ihrer Munterkeit.

Sieht mit Rosen sich umgeben,
Selbst wie eine Rose jung.
Einen Blick, geliebtes Leben!
Und ich bin belohnt genung.

the night created a thousand monsters,
but my spirits were fresh and happy:
in my veins what fire!
In my heart what a blaze!

I saw you, and gentle joy
flowed to me from your sweet glance;
my whole heart was by your side
and my every breath was for you.
A rose-colored springtime atmosphere
encircled your lovely face,
and tenderness toward me—you gods!
I hoped for it, but didn't deserve it!

But alas, as soon as the morning sun rose,
parting constricted my heart:
in your kisses what rapture!
In your eyes what pain!
I went, you stood looking down at the ground
and watched me go with moist eyes:
and yet, what happiness to be loved!
And to love, gods, what happiness!

## With a Painted Ribbon

Kindly young gods of springtime playfully
sprinkle flowers and little leaves
for me with a light hand
onto an airy ribbon.

Zephyr, take it upon your wings,
and tie it around my sweetheart's dress!
And so she will step before her mirror
in all her sprightliness.

She will see herself surrounded by roses,
she herself young as a rose.
Cast me a glance, my love, my life,
and I will be sufficiently repaid.

Fühle, was dies Herz empfindet,
Reiche frei mir deine Hand,
Und das Band, das uns verbindet,
Sei kein schwaches Rosenband!

## Mailied

Wie herrlich leuchtet
Mir die Natur!
Wie glänzt die Sonne!
Wie lacht die Flur!

Es dringen Blüten
Aus jedem Zweig
Und tausend Stimmen
Aus dem Gesträuch,

Und Freud und Wonne
Aus jeder Brust.
O Erd, o Sonne!
O Glück, o Lust!

O Lieb, o Liebe!
So golden schön,
Wie Morgenwolken
Auf jenen Höhn!

Du segnest herrlich
Das frische Feld,
Im Blütendampfe
Die volle Welt.

O Mädchen, Mädchen,
Wie lieb ich dich!
Wie blickt dein Auge!
Wie liebst du mich!

Feel what my heart is experiencing,
give me your hand freely,
and may the tie that unites us
not be a weak ribbon of roses!

## *May Song*

How splendidly nature
gleams for me!
How the sun shines!
How the meadow laughs!

Blossoms burst forth
out of every bough,
and a thousand voices
out of the bushes,

and joy and rapture
out of every breast.
O earth, O sun!
O happiness, O pleasure!

O love, O love!
As golden and beautiful
as morning clouds
on yonder heights!

You splendidly bless
the fresh fields,
the whole world
in the vapor of blossoms.

O my girl, my girl,
how I love you!
What glances your eyes give!
How you love me!

So liebt die Lerche
Gesang und Luft,
Und Morgenblumen
Den Himmelsduft,

Wie ich dich liebe
Mit warmem Blut,
Die du mir Jugend
Und Freud und Mut

Zu neuen Liedern
Und Tänzen gibst.
Sei ewig glücklich,
Wie du mich liebst!

## Heidenröslein

Sah ein Knab ein Röslein stehn,
Röslein auf der Heiden,
War so jung und morgenschön,
Lief er schnell, es nah zu sehn,
Sahs mit vielen Freuden.
Röslein, Röslein, Röslein rot,
Röslein auf der Heiden.

Knabe sprach: Ich breche dich,
Röslein auf der Heiden!
Röslein sprach: Ich steche dich,
Daß du ewig denkst an mich,
Und ich wills nicht leiden.
Röslein, Röslein, Röslein rot,
Röslein auf der Heiden.

Und der wilde Knabe brach
's Röslein auf der Heiden;
Röslein wehrte sich und stach,
Half ihm doch kein Weh und Ach,
Mußt es eben leiden.
Röslein, Röslein, Röslein rot,
Röslein auf der Heiden.

Just so does the lark love
song and sky,
and morning flowers
the heavenly haze,

as I love you
with hot blood,
you who give me youth
and joy and courage

for new songs
and dances.
Be forever happy,
loving me this way!

## Little Rose on the Heath

A lad saw a little rose standing,
little rose on the heath;
it was so young and of such morning beauty,
he ran quickly to see it closely,
he saw it with great joy.
Little rose, rose, red rose,
little rose on the heath.

The lad said: "I shall pluck you,
little rose on the heath!"
The little rose said: "I shall prick you,
so that you remember me forever,
and I won't endure it."
Little rose, rose, red rose,
little rose on the heath.

And the impetuous lad plucked
the little rose on the heath;
the little rose defended itself and pricked him,
but no "woe" or "alas" did it any good;
it just had to endure it.
Little rose, rose, red rose,
little rose on the heath.

## Wanderers Sturmlied

Wen du nicht verlässest, Genius,
Nicht der Regen, nicht der Sturm
Haucht ihm Schauer übers Herz.
Wen du nicht verlässest, Genius,
Wird dem Regengewölk,
Wird dem Schloßensturm
Entgegensingen,
Wie die Lerche,
Du da droben.

Den du nicht verlässest, Genius,
Wirst ihn heben übern Schlammpfad
Mit den Feuerflügeln.
Wandeln wird er
Wie mit Blumenfüßen
Über Deukalions Flutschlamm,
Python tötend, leicht, groß,
Pythius Apollo.

Den du nicht verlässest, Genius,
Wirst die wollnen Flügel unterspreiten,
Wenn er auf dem Felsen schläft,
Wirst mit Hüterfittichen ihn decken
In des Haines Mitternacht.

Wen du nicht verlässest, Genius,
Wirst im Schneegestöber
Wärmumhüllen;
Nach der Wärme ziehn sich Musen,
Nach der Wärme Charitinnen.

Umschwebet mich, ihr Musen,
Ihr Charitinnen!
Das ist Wasser, das ist Erde,
Und der Sohn des Wassers und der Erde,
Über den ich wandle
Göttergleich.

## Wayfarer's Storm Song

The man whom you do not abandon, inborn ability,
neither rain nor storm
can breathe fear into his heart.
The man whom you do not abandon, inborn ability,
will sing in the face of the rain clouds,
in the face of the hailstorm,
he will sing
like the lark,
like you up there.

The one whom you do not abandon, inborn ability,
you will lift him over the miry path
on your wings of fire.
He will walk
as if on flowery feet
over the mire left by Deucalion's flood,
slaying Python, easily, greatly,
a Pythius Apollo.

The one whom you do not abandon, inborn ability,
you will spread your woolly wings under him
when he sleeps on the crag,
you will cover him with protective pinions
in the midnight of the grove.

The man whom you do not abandon, inborn ability,
you will wrap him around warmly
in the snow flurry;
the Muses are drawn toward warmth,
the Graces toward warmth.

Hover around me, Muses,
Graces!
This is water, this is earth,
and the son of water and earth,
over which I walk
like a god.

Ihr seid rein wie das Herz der Wasser,
Ihr seid rein wie das Mark der Erde,
Ihr umschwebt mich, und ich schwebe
Über Wasser, über Erde,
Göttergleich.

Soll der zurückkehren,
Der kleine, schwarze, feurige Bauer?
Soll der zurückkehren, erwartend
Nur deine Gaben, Vater Bromius,
Und helleuchtend umwärmend Feuer?
Der kehren mutig?
Und ich, den ihr begleitet,
Musen und Charitinnen alle,
Den alles erwartet, was ihr,
Musen und Charitinnen,
Umkränzende Seligkeit,
Rings ums Leben verherrlicht habt,
Soll mutlos kehren?

Vater Bromius!
Du bist Genius,
Jahrhunderts Genius,
Bist, was innre Glut
Pindarn war,
Was der Welt
Phöbus Apoll ist.

Weh! Weh! Innre Wärme,
Seelenwärme,
Mittelpunkt!
Glüh entgegen
Phöb Apollen!
Kalt wird sonst
Sein Fürstenblick
Über dich vorübergleiten,
Neidgetroffen
Auf der Zeder Kraft verweilen,
Die zu grünen
Sein nicht harrt.

You are pure as the heart of the waters,
you are pure as the marrow of the earth,
you hover around me, and I hover
over water, over earth,
like a god.

Shall he return home,
that small, dark, fiery peasant?
Shall he return home, awaiting
only your gifts, Father Bromius,
and a brightly glowing, thoroughly warming fire?
Shall he return confidently?
And shall I, whom you are escorting,
all you Muses and Graces,
I, who am awaited by everything that you
Muses and Graces,
you encircling bliss,
have glorified round about my life—
shall I return discouraged?

Father Bromius,
you are the guiding spirit,
the spirit of the century;
you are what his inner glow
was to Pindar,
what Phoebus Apollo is
to the world.

Alas! Alas! Inner warmth,
warmth of the soul,
center point!
Glow in greeting
to Phoebus Apollo!
Or else his princely gaze
will pass by
over you coldly;
stricken by envy,
it will tarry over the strength of the cedar,
which, in order to be green,
does not wait for him.

Warum nennt mein Lied dich zuletzt?
Dich, von dem es begann,
Dich, in dem es endet,
Dich, aus dem es quillt,
Jupiter Pluvius!
Dich, dich strömt mein Lied,
Und kastalischer Quell
Rinnt ein Nebenbach,
Rinnet Müßigen,
Sterblich Glücklichen
Abseits von dir,
Der du mich fassend deckst,
Jupiter Pluvius!

Nicht am Ulmenbaum
Hast du ihn besucht,
Mit dem Taubenpaar
In dem zärtlichen Arm,
Mit der freundlichen Ros umkränzt,
Tändelnden ihn, blumenglücklichen
Anakreon,
Sturmatmende Gottheit!

Nicht im Pappelwald
An des Sybaris Strand,
An des Gebirgs
Sonnebeglänzter Stirn nicht
Faßtest du ihn,
Den Blumen-singenden,
Honig-lallenden,
Freundlich winkenden
Theokrit.

Wenn die Räder rasselten,
Rad an Rad rasch ums Ziel weg,
Hoch flog
Siegdurchglühter
Jünglinge Peitschenknall,
Und sich Staub wälzt',
Wie vom Gebirg herab
Kieselwetter ins Tal,

Why does my song name you last?—
You, with whom it began,
you, with whom it ends,
you, from whom it springs,
Jupiter Pluvius!
It is you, you that my song pours out,
and the Castalian spring
runs along like a tributary brook,
runs along for idlers,
for men who are happy but mortal,
far from you,
you who grasp me and protect me,
Jupiter Pluvius!

You did not visit him
by the elm tree,
with a pair of doves
in his delicate arms,
garlanded with the friendly rose,
playful, happy with his flowers,
you did not visit Anacreon,
storm-breathing deity!

You did not seize him
in the poplar forest
by the shore of Sybaris,
or by the mountain's
sun-illuminated brow,
the singer of flowers,
the prattler of honey,
the amiably beckoning
Theocritus.

When the wheels clattered,
wheel after wheel swiftly rounding the goalpost,
when the whip crack
of young men seared with victory
flew high,
and when dust rolled
like a hailstorm from the mountains
down into the valley,

Glühte deine Seel Gefahren, Pindar,
Mut. – Glühte? –
Armes Herz!
Dort auf dem Hügel,
Himmlische Macht!
Nur so viel Glut,
Dort meine Hütte,
Dorthin zu waten!

## Zigeunerlied

Im Nebelgeriesel, im tiefen Schnee,
Im wilden Wald, in der Winternacht,
Ich hörte der Wölfe Hungergeheul,
Ich hörte der Eulen Geschrei.
   Wille wau wau wau!
     Wille wo wo wo!
     Wito hu!

Ich schoß einmal eine Katz am Zaun,
Der Anne, der Hex, ihre schwarze liebe Katz.
Da kamen des Nachts sieben Werwölf zu mir,
Waren sieben sieben Weiber vom Dorf.
   Wille wau wau wau!
     Wille wo wo wo!
     Wito hu!

Ich kannte sie all, ich kannte sie wohl,
Die Anne, die Ursel, die Käth,
Die Liese, die Barbe, die Ev, die Beth,
Sie heulten im Kreise mich an.
   Wille wau wau wau!
     Wille wo wo wo!
     Wito hu!

Da nannt ich sie alle bei Namen laut:
Was willst du, Anne? was willst du, Beth?
Da rüttelten sie sich, da schüttelten sie sich,
Und liefen und heulten davon.
   Wille wau wau wau!
     Wille wo wo wo!
     Wito hu!

then, Pindar, your soul radiated the warmth of courage
in the face of dangers.—Warmth?—
Poor heart!
There on the hill,
heavenly power,
grant me just enough warmth
to wade over yonder
to my cabin!

## Gypsy Song

In the trickle of mist, in the deep snow,
in the wild forest, in the winter night,
I heard the wolves' howl of hunger,
I heard the cry of the owls.
   Wille wau wau wau!
     Wille wo wo wo!
      Wito hu!

Once I shot a cat by the fence,
the witch Anne's darling black cat.
Then seven werewolves came to me at night,
they were seven, seven women from the village.
   Wille wau wau wau!
     Wille wo wo wo!
      Wito hu!

I knew them all, I knew them well,
Anne, Ursula, Kate,
Liz, Barbara, Eva, Beth,
they stood in a circle howling at me.
   Wille wau wau wau!
     Wille wo wo wo!
      Wito hu!

Then I called them all by name aloud:
"What do you want, Anne? What do you want, Beth?"
Then they shook, then they quivered,
and ran away howling.
   Wille wau wau wau!
     Wille wo wo wo!
      Wito hu!

## Mahomets Gesang

Seht den Felsenquell,
Freudehell,
Wie ein Sternenblick!
Über Wolken
Nährten seine Jugend
Gute Geister
Zwischen Klippen im Gebüsch.

Jünglingfrisch
Tanzt er aus der Wolke
Auf die Marmorfelsen nieder,
Jauchzet wieder
Nach dem Himmel.

Durch die Gipfelgänge
Jagt er bunten Kieseln nach,
Und mit frühem Führertritt
Reißt er seine Bruderquellen
Mit sich fort.

Drunten werden in dem Tal
Unter seinem Fußtritt Blumen,
Und die Wiese
Lebt von seinem Hauch.

Doch ihn hält kein Schattental,
Keine Blumen,
Die ihm seine Knie umschlingen,
Ihm mit Liebes-Augen schmeicheln:
Nach der Ebne dringt sein Lauf
Schlangenwandelnd.

Bäche schmiegen
Sich gesellig an. Nun tritt er
In die Ebne silberprangend,
Und die Ebne prangt mit ihm,
Und die Flüsse von der Ebne

## *Hymn of Mohammed*

See the mountain brook,
joyfully bright,
like a flash of starlight!
Above the clouds
kindly spirits
nourished his youth
between cliffs in the bushes.

With a young man's energy
he dances out of the clouds
down onto the marble rocks,
again rejoicing
to heaven.

Through the passages on the peaks
he hunts after multicolored pebbles,
and with the pace of a youthful leader
he tears his fellow brooks
along with him.

Down in the valley
flowers spring up beneath his feet,
and the meadow
takes life from his breath.

But no shady valley can keep him,
no flowers
that encircle his knees,
flattering him with eyes of love:
his impetus drives him toward the plain,
winding like a snake.

Streams join forces with him,
keeping him company. Now he emerges
onto the plain in silvery splendor,
and the plain is resplendent in him,
and the rivers from the plain

Und die Bäche von den Bergen
Jauchzen ihm und rufen: Bruder!
Bruder, nimm die Brüder mit,
Mit zu deinem alten Vater,
Zu dem ewgen Ozean,
Der mit ausgespannten Armen
Unser wartet,
Die sich, ach! vergebens öffnen,
Seine Sehnenden zu fassen;
Denn uns frißt in öder Wüste
Gierger Sand; die Sonne droben
Saugt an unserm Blut; ein Hügel
Hemmet uns zum Teiche! Bruder,
Nimm die Brüder von der Ebne,
Nimm die Brüder von den Bergen
Mit, zu deinem Vater mit!

Kommt ihr alle! –
Und nun schwillt er
Herrlicher; ein ganz Geschlechte
Trägt den Fürsten hoch empor!
Und im rollenden Triumphe
Gibt er Ländern Namen, Städte
Werden unter seinem Fuß.

Unaufhaltsam rauscht er weiter,
Läßt der Türme Flammengipfel,
Marmorhäuser, eine Schöpfung
Seiner Fülle, hinter sich.

Zedernhäuser trägt der Atlas
Auf den Riesenschultern; sausend
Wehen über seinem Haupte
Tausend Flaggen durch die Lüfte,
Zeugen seiner Herrlichkeit.

Und so trägt er seine Brüder,
Seine Schätze, seine Kinder
Dem erwartenden Erzeuger
Freudebrausend an das Herz!

and the streams from the mountains
shout to him joyfully, calling: "Brother,
brother, take your brothers along,
along to your ancient father,
to the eternal ocean,
who awaits us
with outstretched arms,
which, alas, open in vain
to receive those who long for him;
for we are consumed in the lonely desert
by greedy sands; the sun up above
sucks at our blood; a hill
closes us in and forms a pool! Brother,
take your brothers from the plain,
take your brothers from the mountains
along, along to your father!"

"Come, all of you!"
And now he swells
more splendidly; an entire clan
bears its prince high aloft!
And in his rolling triumphant march
he gives countries their names, cities
spring up beneath his feet.

Unstoppable, he roars onward,
leaving the glowing summits of towers,
marble houses, a creation
of his abundance, far behind him.

This Atlas bears cedar houses
on his gigantic shoulders; rustling,
a thousand banners blow
through the air over his head,
witnesses to his magnificence.

And so he carries his brothers,
his treasures, his children,
roaring with joy, to the heart
of his awaiting begetter!

## Das Veilchen

Ein Veilchen auf der Wiese stand
Gebückt in sich und unbekannt;
Es war ein herzigs Veilchen.
Da kam eine junge Schäferin
Mit leichtem Schritt und munterm Sinn
Daher, daher,
Die Wiese her, und sang.

Ach! denkt das Veilchen, wär ich nur
Die schönste Blume der Natur,
Ach, nur ein kleines Weilchen,
Bis mich das Liebchen abgepflückt
Und an dem Busen matt gedrückt!
Ach nur, ach nur
Ein Viertelstündchen lang!

Ach! aber ach! das Mädchen kam
Und nicht in acht das Veilchen nahm,
Ertrat das arme Veilchen.
Es sank und starb und freut' sich noch:
Und sterb ich denn, so sterb ich doch
Durch sie, durch sie,
Zu ihren Füßen doch.

## Der untreue Knabe

Es war ein Knabe frech genung,
War erst aus Frankreich kommen,
Der hatt ein armes Mädel jung
Gar oft in Arm genommen
Und liebgekost und liebgeherzt,
Als Bräutigam herumgescherzt,
Und endlich sie verlassen.

Das braune Mädel das erfuhr,
Vergingen ihr die Sinnen.

## The Violet

A violet stood in the meadow,
its head bent modestly, unknown to the world;
it was a dear little violet.
There came a young shepherdess
with light steps and lively thoughts
that way, that way,
through the meadow, singing.

"Ah!" thought the violet, "if I were only
the most beautiful flower in nature,
oh, just for a little while,
until my darling picks me
and crushes me against her bosom!
Oh, only, oh, only
for a quarter of an hour!"

Ah, but ah, the girl came by
and failed to notice the violet;
she stepped on the poor violet.
It sank and died, but was still happy:
"And even if I die, I am dying
by her doing, by her doing,
at her feet after all."

## The Faithless Lad

There was a lad who was quite wild,
he had just come from France;
he had very often held in his arms
a poor young girl,
cuddling and caressing her,
sporting with her as a bridegroom would,
and had finally abandoned her.

The dark-complexioned girl heard about that,
and lost her senses.

Sie lacht' und weint' und bet't' und schwur;
So fuhr die Seel von hinnen.
Die Stund, da sie verschieden war,
Wird bang dem Buben, graust sein Haar,
Es treibt ihn fort zu Pferde.

Er gab die Sporen kreuz und quer
Und ritt auf alle Seiten,
Herüber, hinüber, hin und her,
Kann keine Ruh erreiten;
Reit't sieben Tag und sieben Nacht:
Es blitzt und donnert, stürmt und kracht,
Die Fluten reißen über.

Und reit't in Blitz und Wetterschein
Gemäuerwerk entgegen,
Bindt 's Pferd hauß' an und kriecht hinein
Und duckt sich vor dem Regen.
Und wie er tappt, und wie er fühlt,
Sich unter ihm die Erd erwühlt;
Er stürzt wohl hundert Klafter.

Und als er sich ermannt vom Schlag,
Sieht er drei Lichtlein schleichen.
Er rafft sich auf und krabbelt nach;
Die Lichtlein ferne weichen,
Irrführen ihn die Quer und Läng,
Trepp auf, Trepp ab, durch enge Gäng,
Verfallne wüste Keller.

Auf einmal steht er hoch im Saal,
Sieht sitzen hundert Gäste,
Hohläugig grinsen allzumal
Und winken ihm zum Feste.
Er sieht sein Schätzel untenan
Mit weißen Tüchern angetan,
Die wend't sich —

She laughed and cried and prayed and swore oaths;
and so her soul departed.
At the hour when she perished,
the boy became frightened, his hair stood on end;
he felt compelled to ride away.

He spurred his horse this way and that,
riding in all directions,
here, there, back and forth,
but could attain no repose by riding;
he rides seven days and seven nights:
there is lightning and thunder, there is storming and crashing,
the rivers overflow their banks.

And he rides in the lightning and storm glow
toward a masonry building;
he ties up his horse outside and crawls in,
cowering in the rain.
And as he gropes, and as he feels his way,
the earth beneath him gives way violently;
he plunges some hundred fathoms.

And when he recovers from the impact,
he sees three little lights moving quietly.
He pulls himself together and crawls after them;
the lights move away in the distance,
leading him astray this way and that,
up stairs, down stairs, through narrow passages
and chaotic, fallen-in cellars.

All at once he is standing erect in a great hall,
he sees a hundred guests seated there;
they all grin at him with hollow eyes
and bid him join the banquet.
He sees his sweetheart at the far end of the table,
dressed in white clothes;
she turns—

## *Der König in Thule*

Es war ein König in Thule
Gar treu bis an das Grab,
Dem sterbend seine Buhle
Einen goldnen Becher gab.

Es ging ihm nichts darüber,
Er leert' ihn jeden Schmaus;
Die Augen gingen ihm über,
Sooft er trank daraus.

Und als er kam zu sterben,
Zählt' er seine Städt' im Reich,
Gönnt' alles seinen Erben,
Den Becher nicht zugleich.

Er saß beim Königsmahle,
Die Ritter um ihn her,
Auf hohem Vätersaale,
Dort auf dem Schloß am Meer.

Dort stand der alte Zecher,
Trank letzte Lebensglut,
Und warf den heilgen Becher
Hinunter in die Flut.

Er sah ihn stürzen, trinken
Und sinken tief ins Meer.
Die Augen täten ihm sinken;
Trank nie einen Tropfen mehr.

## *Ganymed*

Wie im Morgenglanze
Du rings mich anglühst,
Frühling, Geliebter!
Mit tausendfacher Liebeswonne
Sich an mein Herz drängt

## *The King in Thule*

There was a king in Thule,
completely faithful until the grave,
to whom his mistress, when she was dying,
gave a golden goblet.

He valued nothing more than that,
he drained it at every feast;
his eyes filled with tears
whenever he drank from it.

And when his end was near,
he counted up the cities in his kingdom,
and gladly made everything over to his heirs,
but not the goblet.

He sat at the royal meal,
his knights around him,
in his high-ceilinged ancestral hall,
there in his palace by the sea.

There the old toper stood,
drank the last warmth of life,
and threw the sacred goblet
down into the waves.

He saw it plunge, fill with water,
and sink deep into the sea.
His eyes fell shut;
he never drank another drop.

## *Ganymede*

How in the brightness of morning
you beam on me all around,
springtime, beloved!
With a thousandfold loving rapture
there presses on my heart

Deiner ewigen Wärme
Heilig Gefühl,
Unendliche Schöne!

Daß ich dich fassen möcht
In diesen Arm!

Ach, an deinem Busen
Lieg ich, schmachte,
Und deine Blumen, dein Gras
Drängen sich an mein Herz.
Du kühlst den brennenden
Durst meines Busens,
Lieblicher Morgenwind!
Ruft drein die Nachtigall
Liebend nach mir aus dem Nebeltal.

Ich komm, ich komme!
Wohin? Ach, wohin?
Hinauf! Hinauf strebts.
Es schweben die Wolken
Abwärts, die Wolken
Neigen sich der sehnenden Liebe.
Mir! Mir!
In euerm Schoße
Aufwärts!
Umfangend umfangen!
Aufwärts an deinen Busen,
Alliebender Vater!

## An Schwager Kronos

Spude dich, Kronos!
Fort den rasselnden Trott!
Bergab gleitet der Weg;
Ekles Schwindeln zögert
Mir vor die Stirne dein Haudern.

the holy feeling
of your eternal warmth,
infinite beauty!

So that I would like to grasp you
in these arms!

Ah, on your breast
I lie, languishing,
and your flowers, your grass
press upon my heart.
You cool the burning
thirst of my breast,
lovely morning breeze!
Meanwhile the nightingale calls
lovingly to me from the misty valley.

I'm coming, I'm coming!
Where to? Ah, where to?
Upward! The striving is upward.
The clouds float
downward, the clouds
incline themselves toward my yearning love.
To me! To me!
In your bosom
upward!
Embracing and embraced!
Upward to your breast,
all-loving Father!

## *To Coachman Kronos*

Hurry up, Kronos!
Onward at a clattering trot!
The road glides downhill;
the hesitancy of your driving causes
nauseating dizziness in my head.

Frisch, holpert es gleich,
Über Stock und Steine den Trott
Rasch ins Leben hinein!

Nun schon wieder
Den eratmenden Schritt
Mühsam Berg hinauf!
Auf denn! nicht träge denn!
Strebend und hoffend hinan!

Weit, hoch, herrlich der Blick
Rings ins Leben hinein!
Vom Gebirg zum Gebirg
Schwebet der ewige Geist,
Ewigen Lebens ahndevoll.

Seitwärts des Überdachs Schatten
Zieht dich an
Und ein Frischung verheißender Blick
Auf der Schwelle des Mädchens da.
Labe dich! – Mir auch, Mädchen,
Diesen schäumenden Trank,
Diesen frischen Gesundheitsblick!

Ab denn, rascher hinab!
Sieh, die Sonne sinkt!
Eh sie sinkt, eh mich Greisen
Ergreift im Moore Nebelduft,
Entzahnte Kiefer schnattern
Und das schlotternde Gebein:

Trunknen vom letzten Strahl
Reiß mich, ein Feuermeer
Mir im schäumenden Aug,
Mich Geblendeten, Taumelnden
In der Hölle nächtliches Tor!

Töne, Schwager, ins Horn,
Raßle den schallenden Trab,
Daß der Orkus vernehme: wir kommen!
Daß gleich an der Türe
Der Wirt uns freundlich empfange!

Lively now, even if we get jolted,
move at a trot over stumps and stones
swiftly into life!

Once again now
that heavy-breathing pace
laboriously uphill!
Come now! No laziness!
Upward in striving and in hope!

Far, high, magnificent the view
into life all around us!
From one mountain chain to another
soars the eternal spirit
with a premonition of eternal life.

By the roadside the shade of the overhanging roof
attracts you,
and a glance promising refreshment
from that girl there on the threshold.
Refresh yourself!—For me, too, girl,
that foaming beverage,
that fresh glance of health!

Downward now, more swiftly downward!
See, the sun is setting!
Before it sets, before a misty haze
seizes upon me, an old man, on the moor,
and toothless jaws rattle
and my skeleton shakes:

While I am intoxicated by the last sunbeam,
tear me away, with a sea of fire
in my watery eyes,
tear me away, blinded, staggering,
into the nocturnal gate of hell!

Blow your horn, coachman,
rattle away at a noisy trot,
so that Orcus can hear: we're coming!
So that right at the door
the innkeeper will receive us cheerfully!

## *Prometheus*

Bedecke deinen Himmel, Zeus,
Mit Wolkendunst
Und übe, dem Knaben gleich,
Der Disteln köpft,
An Eichen dich und Bergeshöhn!
Mußt mir meine Erde
Doch lassen stehn
Und meine Hütte, die du nicht gebaut,
Und meinen Herd,
Um dessen Glut
Du mich beneidest.

Ich kenne nichts Ärmeres
Unter der Sonn als euch, Götter!
Ihr nähret kümmerlich
Von Opfersteuern
Und Gebetshauch
Eure Majestät
Und darbtet, wären
Nicht Kinder und Bettler
Hoffnungsvolle Toren.

Da ich ein Kind war,
Nicht wußte, wo aus noch ein,
Kehrt ich mein verirrtes Auge
Zur Sonne, als wenn drüber wär
Ein Ohr, zu hören meine Klage,
Ein Herz wie meins,
Sich des Bedrängten zu erbarmen.

Wer half mir
Wider der Titanen Übermut?
Wer rettete vom Tode mich,
Von Sklaverei?
Hast du nicht alles selbst vollendet,
Heilig glühend Herz?
Und glühtest jung und gut,
Betrogen, Rettungsdank
Dem Schlafenden da droben?

## *Prometheus*

Cover your sky, Zeus,
with cloudy vapor
and, like a boy
who beheads thistles,
practice on oaks and mountain heights!
You nevertheless must
let my earth remain,
and my hut, which you did not build,
and my hearth,
for whose warm fire
you envy me.

I know nothing pettier
under the sun than you, gods!
You meagerly nourish
your majesty
with imposed sacrifices
and the breath of prayers,
and you would starve if
children and beggars
were not fools dependent on hope.

When I was a child,
and did not know one thing from another,
I turned my bewildered eyes
toward the sun, as if up there there was
an ear to hear my lament,
a heart like mine,
to take pity on me when I was hard pressed.

Who aided me
against the arrogance of the Titans?
Who saved me from death,
from slavery?
Did you not accomplish everything yourself,
my sacredly glowing heart?
And, in your youth and goodness,
deceived, did you not warmly give thanks for salvation
to the sleeper up above?

Ich dich ehren? Wofür?
Hast du die Schmerzen gelindert
Je des Beladenen?
Hast du die Tränen gestillet
Je des Geängsteten?
Hat nicht mich zum Manne geschmiedet
Die allmächtige Zeit
Und das ewige Schicksal,
Meine Herrn und deine?

Wähntest du etwa,
Ich sollte das Leben hassen,
In Wüsten fliehen,
Weil nicht alle
Blütenträume reiften?

Hier sitz ich, forme Menschen
Nach meinem Bilde,
Ein Geschlecht, das mir gleich sei,
Zu leiden, zu weinen,
Zu genießen und zu freuen sich,
Und dein nicht zu achten,
Wie ich!

## Neue Liebe neues Leben

Herz, mein Herz, was soll das geben?
Was bedränget dich so sehr?
Welch ein fremdes, neues Leben!
Ich erkenne dich nicht mehr.
Weg ist alles, was du liebtest,
Weg, warum du dich betrübtest,
Weg dein Fleiß und deine Ruh –
Ach, wie kamst du nur dazu!

Fesselt dich die Jugendblüte,
Diese liebliche Gestalt,
Dieser Blick voll Treu und Güte
Mit unendlicher Gewalt?

I honor you? What for?
Have you ever soothed my pains
when I was burdened?
Have you ever stilled my tears
when I was anguished?
Have I not been forged into manhood
by almighty time
and eternal destiny,
my lords and yours?

Did you perhaps imagine
that I was to hate life,
escape into deserts,
because not all
my budding dreams came to fruition?

Here I sit and form people
in my image,
a race that shall be like me,
to suffer, to weep,
to enjoy and to be happy—
and to pay you no mind,
like me!

## New Love, New Life

Heart, my heart, what will come of this?
What oppresses you so greatly?
What an unfamiliar, new life!
I no longer recognize you.
Gone is everything you loved,
gone the cause of your sorrows,
gone your diligence and your peace—
Ah, how did you get this way?

Are you enchained by the youthful blossom,
by this lovely form,
do these eyes full of fidelity and kindness
enchain you with infinite power?

Will ich rasch mich ihr entziehen,
Mich ermannen, ihr entfliehen,
Führet mich im Augenblick,
Ach, mein Weg zu ihr zurück.

Und an diesem Zauberfädchen,
Das sich nicht zerreißen läßt,
Hält das liebe, lose Mädchen
Mich so wider Willen fest;
Muß in ihrem Zauberkreise
Leben nun auf ihre Weise.
Die Verändrung, ach, wie groß!
Liebe! Liebe! laß mich los!

## Auf dem See

Und frische Nahrung, neues Blut
Saug ich aus freier Welt;
Wie ist Natur so hold und gut,
Die mich am Busen hält!
Die Welle wieget unsern Kahn
Im Rudertakt hinauf,
Und Berge, wolkig himmelan,
Begegnen unserm Lauf.

Aug, mein Aug, was sinkst du nieder?
Goldne Träume, kommt ihr wieder?
Weg, du Traum! so gold du bist;
Hier auch Lieb und Leben ist.

Auf der Welle blinken
Tausend schwebende Sterne,
Weiche Nebel trinken
Rings die türmende Ferne;
Morgenwind umflügelt
Die beschattete Bucht,
Und im See bespiegelt
Sich die reifende Frucht.

If I want to withdraw from her swiftly,
to pull myself together, to escape her,
at the very same moment,
alas, my path leads me back to her.

And by this magic thread,
which cannot be torn,
the dear, wanton girl
holds me fast this way against my will;
I must now live as she sees fit
within her magic circle.
Ah, what a great change!
Love, love, let me go!

## On the Lake

And fresh nutriment, new blood
I imbibe from the wide world;
how fair and good is nature,
which holds me to her breast!
The waves rock our boat
upward to the beat of the oars,
and mountains, climbing skyward into the clouds,
come to meet us as we sail.

Eyes, my eyes, why are you downcast?
Golden dreams, are you returning?
Away, you dream, however golden you may be!
Love and life are here too.

On the waves there twinkle
a thousand hovering stars;
soft mists absorb
the towering distance all about;
the morning wind flies around
the shadowed bay,
and in the lake is reflected
the ripening fruit.

## Bundeslied

In allen guten Stunden,
Erhöht von Lieb und Wein,
Soll dieses Lied verbunden
Von uns gesungen sein!
Uns hält der Gott zusammen,
Der uns hierher gebracht.
Erneuert unsre Flammen,
Er hat sie angefacht.

So glühet fröhlich heute,
Seid recht von Herzen eins!
Auf, trinkt erneuter Freude
Dies Glas des echten Weins!
Auf, in der holden Stunde
Stoßt an und küsset treu,
Bei jedem neuen Bunde,
Die alten wieder neu!

Wer lebt in unserm Kreise,
Und lebt nicht selig drin?
Genießt die freie Weise
Und treuen Brudersinn!
So bleibt durch alle Zeiten
Herz Herzen zugekehrt;
Von keinen Kleinigkeiten
Wird unser Bund gestört.

Uns hat ein Gott gesegnet
Mit freiem Lebensblick,
Und alles, was begegnet,
Erneuert unser Glück.
Durch Grillen nicht gedränget,
Verknickt sich keine Lust;
Durch Zieren nicht geenget,
Schlägt freier unsre Brust.

Mit jedem Schritt wird weiter
Die rasche Lebensbahn,
Und heiter, immer heiter
Steigt unser Blick hinan.

# Song of Alliance

At all happy hours,
heightened by love and wine,
may this song
be sung by us in alliance!
We are kept together by the god
who brought us here.
Renew our flames,
it was he who kindled them.

And so glow with merry warmth today,
be as one in your very hearts!
Come, drink to renewed joy
from this glass of genuine wine!
Come, at this fair hour
clink glasses and exchange faithful kisses,
at each new alliance
renewing the old ones!

Who lives in our circle
and doesn't live blissfully within it?
Enjoy our unconstrained ways
and our loyal, fraternal mentality!
And so for all time
each heart will be inclined toward the others;
our alliance isn't disturbed
by any trivial things.

A god has blessed us
with a liberal attitude toward life,
and everything that comes our way
renews our happiness.
Undistressed by caprices,
no pleasure is abated;
unconstricted by ceremony,
our hearts beat more freely.

With every step
the swift course of our life is widened,
and serenely, always serenely,
our gaze mounts upward.

Uns wird es nimmer bange,
Wenn alles steigt und fällt,
Und bleiben lange, lange!
Auf ewig so gesellt.

## Wonne der Wehmut

Trocknet nicht, trocknet nicht,
Tränen der ewigen Liebe!
Ach, nur dem halbgetrockneten Auge
Wie öde, wie tot die Welt ihm erscheint!
Trocknet nicht, trocknet nicht,
Tränen unglücklicher Liebe!

## Jägers Abendlied

Im Felde schleich ich still und wild,
Gespannt mein Feuerrohr.
Da schwebt so licht dein liebes Bild,
Dein süßes Bild mir vor.

Du wandelst jetzt wohl still und mild
Durch Feld und liebes Tal,
Und ach, mein schnell verrauschend Bild,
Stellt sich dirs nicht einmal?

Des Menschen, der die Welt durchstreift
Voll Unmut und Verdruß,
Nach Osten und nach Westen schweift,
Weil er dich lassen muß.

Mir ist es, denk ich nur an dich,
Als in den Mond zu sehn;
Ein stiller Friede kommt auf mich,
Weiß nicht, wie mir geschehn.

We never become frightened
when everything rises and falls,
and for a long, long time—
eternally—we'll remain companions.

## Bliss in Melancholy

Don't dry, don't dry,
tears of eternal love!
Ah, to eyes that are only half dried
how dreary, how dead the world appears!
Don't dry, don't dry,
tears of unhappy love!

## Huntsman's Evening Song

In the fields I stalk about, silently and fiercely,
my gun cocked.
And then your dear image, your sweet image
hovers so brightly before me.

You are now probably walking, silently and gently,
through fields and the lovely valley,
and, ah, does my rapidly vanishing image
not appear before you even once?—

the image of the man who wanders through the world
full of displeasure and vexation,
roaming east and west,
because he must leave you.

Whenever I think of you, I feel
as if I were looking at the moon;
a quiet peace comes over me,
I don't know how it has happened.

## Hoffnung

Schaff, das Tagwerk meiner Hände,
Hohes Glück, daß ichs vollende!
Laß, o laß mich nicht ermatten!
Nein, es sind nicht leere Träume:
Jetzt nur Stangen, diese Bäume
Geben einst noch Frucht und Schatten.

## Wandrers Nachtlied

Der du von dem Himmel bist,
Alles Leid und Schmerzen stillest,
Den, der doppelt elend ist,
Doppelt mit Erquickung füllest,
Ach, ich bin des Treibens müde!
Was soll all der Schmerz und Lust?
Süßer Friede,
Komm, ach komm in meine Brust!

## An Charlotte von Stein

Warum gabst du uns die tiefen Blicke,
Unsre Zukunft ahndungsvoll zu schaun,
Unsrer Liebe, unserm Erdenglücke
Wähnend selig nimmer hinzutraun?
Warum gabst uns, Schicksal, die Gefühle,
Uns einander in das Herz zu sehn,
Um durch all die seltenen Gewühle
Unser wahr Verhältnis auszuspähn?

Ach, so viele tausend Menschen kennen,
Dumpf sich treibend, kaum ihr eigen Herz,
Schweben zwecklos hin und her und rennen
Hoffnungslos in unversehnen Schmerz;
Jauchzen wieder, wenn der schnellen Freuden
Unerwart'te Morgenröte tagt.

## *Hope*

Great good fortune, bring it about
that I may complete the daily task of my hands!
Let, oh, let me not grow weary!
No, these are no empty dreams:
mere sticks now, these trees
will one day give fruit and shade.

## *Wayfarer's Night Song*

You who are from heaven
and soothe all sorrow and pains,
filling doubly with relief
the man who is doubly miserable,
ah, I am weary of this toil!
What is the meaning of all the pain and pleasure?
Sweet peace,
come, oh, come to my breast!

## *To Charlotte von Stein*

Why did you give us the deep insight
enabling us to see hints of our future,
so that we can no longer, in a blissful delusion,
trust our love, our earthly happiness?
Why, fate, did you give us feelings
enabling us to read each other's hearts
in order to spy out our true situation
amid all the strange turmoils?

Ah, so many thousands of people,
drifting insensibly, scarcely know their own heart,
but float aimlessly here and there and dash
hopelessly into unforeseen pain,
rejoicing once more when the unexpected dawn
of rapidly fleeting joys breaks.

Nur uns armen liebevollen Beiden
Ist das wechselseitge Glück versagt,
Uns zu lieben, ohn uns zu verstehen,
In dem andern sehn, was er nie war,
Immer frisch auf Traumglück auszugehen
Und zu schwanken auch in Traumgefahr.

Glücklich, den ein leerer Traum beschäftigt!
Glücklich, dem die Ahndung eitel wär!
Jede Gegenwart und jeder Blick bekräftigt
Traum und Ahndung leider uns noch mehr.
Sag, was will das Schicksal uns bereiten?
Sag, wie band es uns so rein genau?
Ach, du warst in abgelebten Zeiten
Meine Schwester oder meine Frau.

Kanntest jeden Zug in meinem Wesen,
Spähtest, wie die reinste Nerve klingt,
Konntest mich mit Einem Blicke lesen,
Den so schwer ein sterblich Aug durchdringt;
Tropftest Mäßigung dem heißen Blute,
Richtetest den wilden irren Lauf,
Und in deinen Engelsarmen ruhte
Die zerstörte Brust sich wieder auf;
Hieltest zauberleicht ihn angebunden
Und vergaukeltest ihm manchen Tag.
Welche Seligkeit glich jenen Wonnestunden,
Da er dankbar dir zu Füßen lag,
Fühlt' sein Herz an deinem Herzen schwellen,
Fühlte sich in deinem Auge gut,
Alle seine Sinnen sich erhellen
Und beruhigen sein brausend Blut!

Und von allem dem schwebt ein Erinnern
Nur noch um das ungewisse Herz,
Fühlt die alte Wahrheit ewig gleich im Innern,
Und der neue Zustand wird ihm Schmerz.
Und wir scheinen uns nur halb beseelet,
Dämmernd ist um uns der hellste Tag.
Glücklich, daß das Schicksal, das uns quälet,
Uns doch nicht verändern mag!

Only we two poor lovers
are denied the mutual happiness
of loving each other without understanding each other,
of seeing in each other something we never were,
of setting out to find a dreamer's happiness again and again,
and also of wavering in the danger of dreams.

Happy the man who is occupied by an idle dream!
Happy the man whose premonition might be false!
Unfortunately, in our case, every meeting and every glance
only confirms our dreams and portents all the more.
Tell me, what will fate have in store for us?
Tell me, how did it bind us together so perfectly tight?
Ah, in ages long past you were
my sister or my wife.

You knew every trait in my nature;
you discovered the sound of my purest strings;
you were able to read me at a glance,
although mortal eyes penetrate me with such difficulty;
you poured drops of moderation into my hot blood;
you regulated my wild, erratic course;
and in your angel's arms
my shattered breast found repose and restoration;
with magical lightness you kept him tied to you
and you charmed away many a day for him.
What bliss equaled those rapturous hours
when he lay at your feet in gratitude,
feeling his heart heaving upon your heart,
feeling that he was worthy in your eyes,
feeling all his senses brightening
and his roaring blood calming down!

And of all that only a reminiscence
still hovers around his uncertain heart;
he feels the old truth eternally the same within him,
and his new condition becomes painful to him.
And we seem to ourselves to be only half alive;
the brightest day is like twilight around us.
Fortunately, the fate that torments us
is nevertheless powerless to change us!

## Rastlose Liebe

Dem Schnee, dem Regen,
Dem Wind entgegen,
Im Dampf der Klüfte,
Durch Nebeldüfte,
Immer zu! Immer zu!
Ohne Rast und Ruh!

Lieber durch Leiden
Möcht ich mich schlagen,
Als so viel Freuden
Des Lebens ertragen.
Alle das Neigen
Von Herzen zu Herzen,
Ach, wie so eigen
Schaffet das Schmerzen!

Wie soll ich fliehen?
Wälderwärts ziehen?
Alles vergebens!
Krone des Lebens,
Glück ohne Ruh,
Liebe, bist du!

## "Alles geben die Götter, die unendlichen"

Alles geben die Götter, die unendlichen,
Ihren Lieblingen ganz,
Alle Freuden, die unendlichen,
Alle Schmerzen, die unendlichen, ganz.

## An den Mond

Füllest wieder Busch und Tal
Still mit Nebelglanz,
Lösest endlich auch einmal
Meine Seele ganz,

## Restless Love

Into the snow, the rain,
the wind,
in the vapor of the chasms,
through misty haze,
onward, onward,
without rest or repose!

I would rather force my way
through sorrows
than to endure so many
joys of life.
All the inclination
of one heart to another,
oh, how oddly
it causes pain!

How shall I flee?
Journey toward the woods?
All in vain!
The crown of life,
happiness without repose:
love, that is what you are!

## "The gods, the infinite ones, give everything"

The gods, the infinite ones, give everything
in its entirety to their favorites,
all joys, the infinite ones,
all pains, the infinite ones, in their entirety.

## To the Moon

Again you fill bush and valley
silently with a misty glow,
and also you finally release
my soul entirely.

Breitest über mein Gefild
Lindernd deinen Blick,
Wie des Freundes Auge mild
Über mein Geschick.

Jeden Nachklang fühlt mein Herz
Froh- und trüber Zeit,
Wandle zwischen Freud und Schmerz
In der Einsamkeit.

Fließe, fließe, lieber Fluß!
Nimmer werd ich froh,
So verrauschte Scherz und Kuß,
Und die Treue so.

Ich besaß es doch einmal,
Was so köstlich ist!
Daß man doch zu seiner Qual
Nimmer es vergißt!

Rausche, Fluß, das Tal entlang,
Ohne Rast und Ruh,
Rausche, flüstre meinem Sang
Melodien zu,

Wenn du in der Winternacht
Wütend überschwillst,
Oder um die Frühlingspracht
Junger Knospen quillst.

Selig, wer sich vor der Welt
Ohne Haß verschließt,
Einen Freund am Busen hält
Und mit dem genießt,

Was, von Menschen nicht gewußt
Oder nicht bedacht,
Durch das Labyrinth der Brust
Wandelt in der Nacht.

You spread your gaze
soothingly over my fields,
like a friend's eyes gently
looking upon my fate.

My heart feels every after-echo
of happy and dreary times,
I walk between joy and pain
in the solitude.

Flow, flow, dear river!
I will never become happy again:
thus merriment and kisses hastened by,
and thus did faithfulness.

But I did once possess
that which is so precious!
To think that nevertheless, to one's torment,
one never forgets it!

Murmur, river, along the valley,
without rest or repose;
murmur, whisper melodies
to my song,

when, in the winter night, you
furiously overflow,
or when you purl around the springtime splendor
of young buds.

Blessed is the man who shuts himself off
from the world without hatred,
clasps a friend to his breast,
and, together with him, enjoys

that which, not known to people
or not considered,
walks through the labyrinth of the heart
in the night.

## Harzreise im Winter

Dem Geier gleich,
Der auf schweren Morgenwolken
Mit sanftem Fittich ruhend
Nach Beute schaut,
Schwebe mein Lied!

Denn ein Gott hat
Jedem seine Bahn
Vorgezeichnet,
Die der Glückliche
Rasch zum freudigen
Ziele rennt:
Wem aber Unglück
Das Herz zusammenzog,
Er sträubt vergebens
Sich gegen die Schranken
Des ehernen Fadens,
Den die doch bittre Schere
Nur einmal löst.

In Dickichts-Schauer
Drängt sich das rauhe Wild,
Und mit den Sperlingen
Haben längst die Reichen
In ihre Sümpfe sich gesenkt.

Leicht ists folgen dem Wagen,
Den Fortuna führt,
Wie der gemächliche Troß
Auf gebesserten Wegen
Hinter des Fürsten Einzug.

Aber abseits wer ists?
Ins Gebüsch verliert sich sein Pfad,
Hinter ihm schlagen
Die Sträuche zusammen,
Das Gras steht wieder auf,
Die Öde verschlingt ihn.

## *Journey to the Harz in Winter*

Like a great bird of prey,
which, resting with gentle pinions
on heavy morning clouds,
looks around for its quarry:
thus let my song soar!

For a god has
predestined
everyone's course,
which the happy man
swiftly races
to its joyous goal:
but the man whose heart
has been constricted by misfortune
beats in vain
against the barriers
of the bronze thread of fate
that only the shears, bitter though they be,
will cut one day.

Into the shelter of the thicket
the rough wild animals are pushing,
and, along with the reed warblers,
the rich folk have long since
submerged into their swamps.

It is easy to follow the chariot
that Fortuna leads,
just as the easy-paced pack train
follows after the prince's entry
on improved roads.

But, off the path there, who is that?
His trail is lost in the shrubbery;
behind him the bushes
close up,
the grass springs up again,
the wilderness swallows him up.

Ach, wer heilet die Schmerzen
Des, dem Balsam zu Gift ward?
Der sich Menschenhaß
Aus der Fülle der Liebe trank?
Erst verachtet, nun ein Verächter,
Zehrt er heimlich auf
Seinen eignen Wert
In ungnügender Selbstsucht.

Ist auf deinem Psalter,
Vater der Liebe, ein Ton
Seinem Ohre vernehmlich,
So erquicke sein Herz!
Öffne den umwölkten Blick
Über die tausend Quellen
Neben dem Durstenden
In der Wüste!

Der du der Freuden viel schaffst,
Jedem ein überfließend Maß,
Segne die Brüder der Jagd
Auf der Fährte des Wilds
Mit jugendlichem Übermut
Fröhlicher Mordsucht,
Späte Rächer des Unbills,
Dem schon Jahre vergeblich
Wehrt mit Knütteln der Bauer!

Aber den Einsamen hüll
In deine Goldwolken!
Umgib mit Wintergrün,
Bis die Rose wieder heranreift,
Die feuchten Haare,
O Liebe, deines Dichters!

Mit der dämmernden Fackel
Leuchtest du ihm
Durch die Furten bei Nacht,
Über grundlose Wege
Auf öden Gefilden;

Ah, who will heal the pains
of a man for whom balm has become poison,
a man who imbibed misanthropy
from the abundance of love?
Formerly despised, now a despiser,
he secretly consumes
his own worth
in unsatisfying egotism.

If your psaltery,
Father of love, possesses a tone
perceptible to his ears,
then refresh his heart!
Open his clouded eyes
to the thousand fountains
alongside the parched man
in the desert!

You who provide many joys,
an overflowing measure for everyone,
bless the brothers of the chase
on their track of game
with the youthful exuberance
of merry blood lust:
belated avengers of the damage
that for years now, in vain,
the peasant has warded off with cudgels!

But envelop the solitary wayfarer
in your golden clouds!
Encircle with wintergreen,
until the rose is again ready to blossom,
the damp hair
of your poet, O Love!

With your twilight torch
you light his way
through fords at night,
over bottomless precipices
on barren stretches of ground;

Mit dem tausendfarbigen Morgen
Lachst du ins Herz ihm;
Mit dem beizenden Sturm
Trägst du ihn hoch empor;
Winterströme stürzen vom Felsen
In seine Psalmen,
Und Altar des lieblichsten Danks
Wird ihm des gefürchteten Gipfels
Schneebehangner Scheitel,
Den mit Geisterreihen
Kränzten ahnende Völker.

Du stehst mit unerforschtem Busen
Geheimnisvoll offenbar
Über der erstaunten Welt
Und schaust aus Wolken
Auf ihre Reiche und Herrlichkeit,
Die du aus den Adern deiner Brüder
Neben dir wässerst.

## Der Fischer

Das Wasser rauscht', das Wasser schwoll,
Ein Fischer saß daran,
Sah nach dem Angel ruhevoll,
Kühl bis ans Herz hinan.
Und wie er sitzt und wie er lauscht,
Teilt sich die Flut empor;
Aus dem bewegten Wasser rauscht
Ein feuchtes Weib hervor.

Sie sang zu ihm, sie sprach zu ihm:
Was lockst du meine Brut
Mit Menschenwitz und Menschenlist
Hinauf in Todesglut?
Ach wüßtest du, wie's Fischlein ist
So wohlig auf dem Grund,
Du stiegst herunter, wie du bist,
Und würdest erst gesund!

with the thousand-colored morning
you smile into his heart;
with the corrosive storm
you bear him high aloft;
wintry streams plunge from the cliffs
into his psalms,
and he finds an altar for dearest thanksgiving
in the snow-hung summit
of the dreaded peak
that, in the visions of people of old,
was garlanded by ghostly round dances.

You, peak, with your unexplored bosom, stand
mysteriously apparent
above the astonished world
and look down from the clouds
upon its kingdoms and magnificence,
which you irrigate from the veins
of your brothers alongside you.

## The Fisherman

The water rushed, the water rose;
a fisherman sat by it,
looking peacefully at his rod,
cool to the depths of his heart.
And as he sits and as he listens,
the waves separate upward:
from the agitated water there swiftly emerges
a woman of the deeps.

She sang to him, she spoke to him:
"Why do you lure my brood
with human intelligence and human guile
up into the heat of death?
Ah, if you knew how comfortable
the little fishes are down at the bottom,
you would descend just as you are,
and would become hale for the first time.

Labt sich die liebe Sonne nicht,
Der Mond sich nicht im Meer?
Kehrt wellenatmend ihr Gesicht
Nicht doppelt schöner her?
Lockt dich der tiefe Himmel nicht,
Das feuchtverklärte Blau?
Lockt dich dein eigen Angesicht
Nicht her in ewgen Tau?

Das Wasser rauscht', das Wasser schwoll,
Netzt' ihm den nackten Fuß;
Sein Herz wuchs ihm so sehnsuchtsvoll,
Wie bei der Liebsten Gruß.
Sie sprach zu ihm, sie sang zu ihm;
Da wars um ihn geschehn:
Halb zog sie ihn, halb sank er hin,
Und ward nicht mehr gesehn.

## Grenzen der Menschheit

Wenn der uralte,
Heilige Vater
Mit gelassener Hand
Aus rollenden Wolken
Segnende Blitze
Über die Erde sät,
Küß ich den letzten
Saum seines Kleides,
Kindliche Schauer
Treu in der Brust.

Denn mit Göttern
Soll sich nicht messen
Irgendein Mensch.
Hebt er sich aufwärts
Und berührt
Mit dem Scheitel die Sterne,
Nirgends haften dann
Die unsichern Sohlen,
Und mit ihm spielen
Wolken und Winde.

"Does not the dear sun,
does not the moon refresh itself in the sea?
Does not their face, breathing the waves,
return from here doubly beautiful?
Does not the heaven of the depths lure you,
the blueness transfigured by the liquid?
Does not your own countenance lure you
down here to the eternal dew?"

The water rushed, the water rose,
wetting his naked foot;
his heart expanded as longingly
as if his sweetheart had greeted him.
She spoke to him, she sang to him,
then his doom was sealed:
partly she drew him in, partly he let himself sink,
and was never seen again.

## Limitations of Humanity

When the ancient
Holy Father
with calm hand
sows beneficent lightnings
from rolling clouds
onto the earth,
I kiss the nethermost
hem of his garment,
with childlike thrills
loyally in my heart.

For no man
should measure himself
against gods.
If he raises himself upward
and touches
the stars with the crown of his head,
then nowhere
do his unstable feet find a hold,
and clouds and winds
make him their plaything.

Steht er mit festen,
Markigen Knochen
Auf der wohlgegründeten
Dauernden Erde,
Reicht er nicht auf,
Nur mit der Eiche
Oder der Rebe
Sich zu vergleichen.

Was unterscheidet
Götter von Menschen?
Daß viele Wellen
Vor jenen wandeln,
Ein ewiger Strom:
Uns hebt die Welle,
Verschlingt die Welle,
Und wir versinken.

Ein kleiner Ring
Begrenzt unser Leben,
Und viele Geschlechter
Reihen sich dauernd
An ihres Daseins
Unendliche Kette.

## *Gesang der Geister über den Wassern*

Des Menschen Seele
Gleicht dem Wasser:
Vom Himmel kommt es,
Zum Himmel steigt es,
Und wieder nieder
Zur Erde muß es,
Ewig wechselnd.

Strömt von der hohen,
Steilen Felswand
Der reine Strahl,
Dann stäubt er lieblich

If he stands with firm,
vigorous bones
upon the securely established,
enduring earth,
he is unable
to compare himself
with even the oak
or the grapevine.

What distinguishes
gods from men?
It is that many waves
move past the former,
an endless current:
but *we* are tossed by the wave,
swallowed up by the wave,
and we sink.

A small circular link
bounds our life,
and many generations
are continually strung out
on the infinite chain
of their existence.

## Hymn of the Spirits over the Waters

The soul of man
resembles water:
it comes from heaven,
it rises to heaven,
and it must descend
back to earth,
in eternal alternation.

The pure jet
streams from the lofty,
steep rock wall,
then falls as charming droplets

In Wolkenwellen
Zum glatten Fels,
Und leicht empfangen
Wallt er verschleiernd,
Leisrauschend
Zur Tiefe nieder.

Ragen Klippen
Dem Sturz entgegen,
Schäumt er unmutig
Stufenweise
Zum Abgrund.

Im flachen Bette
Schleicht er das Wiesental hin,
Und in dem glatten See
Weiden ihr Antlitz
Alle Gestirne.

Wind ist der Welle
Lieblicher Buhler;
Wind mischt vom Grund aus
Schäumende Wogen.

Seele des Menschen,
Wie gleichst du dem Wasser!
Schicksal des Menschen,
Wie gleichst du dem Wind!

## Liebhaber in allen Gestalten

Ich wollt, ich wär ein Fisch,
So hurtig und frisch;
Und kämst du zu anglen,
Ich würde nicht manglen.
Ich wollt, ich wär ein Fisch,
So hurtig und frisch.

in cloudy waves
to the smooth rock,
and, gently received,
it bubbles with a veil of mist
and a quiet murmur
down to the depths.

If cliffs loom up
to meet its plunge,
it foams indignantly,
in stages,
into the abyss.

In its flat bed
it moves quietly down the meadowy valley,
and in the smooth lake
all the heavenly bodies
cool their faces.

Wind is the wave's
amorous lover;
wind stirs foaming waves
up from the very bottom.

Soul of man,
how you resemble water!
Fate of man,
how you resemble the wind!

## A Lover in All Shapes

I wish I were a fish,
so nimble and lively;
and if you came fishing,
I wouldn't fail to show up.
I wish I were a fish,
so nimble and lively.

Ich wollt, ich wär ein Pferd,
Da wär ich dir wert.
O wär ich ein Wagen,
Bequem dich zu tragen.
Ich wollt, ich wär ein Pferd,
Da wär ich dir wert.

Ich wollt, ich wäre Gold,
Dir immer im Sold;
Und tätst du was kaufen,
Käm ich wieder gelaufen.
Ich wollt, ich wäre Gold,
Dir immer im Sold.

Ich wollt, ich wär treu,
Mein Liebchen stets neu;
Ich wollt mich verheißen,
Wollt nimmer verreisen.
Ich wollt, ich wär treu,
Mein Liebchen stets neu.

Ich wollt, ich wär alt
Und runzlig und kalt;
Tätst du mirs versagen,
Da könnt michs nicht plagen.
Ich wollt, ich wär alt
Und runzlig und kalt.

Wär ich Affe sogleich
Voll neckender Streich;
Hätt was dich verdrossen,
So macht ich dir Possen.
Wär ich Affe sogleich
Voll neckender Streich.

Wär ich gut wie ein Schaf,
Wie der Löwe so brav;
Hätt Augen wie's Lüchschen
Und Listen wie's Füchschen.
Wär ich gut wie ein Schaf,
Wie der Löwe so brav.

I wish I were a horse,
then I'd be of value to you.
Oh, if only I were a carriage,
to carry you in comfort.
I wish I were a horse,
then I'd be of value to you.

I wish I were gold,
always at your service;
and if you bought something,
I'd come running back to you.
I wish I were gold,
always at your service.

I wish I were faithful,
always young for my sweetheart;
I would pledge myself to you,
I would never travel away.
I wish I were faithful,
always young for my sweetheart.

I wish I were old
and wrinkled and cold;
if you wouldn't let me have it,
then that couldn't trouble me.
I wish I were old
and wrinkled and cold.

If I could only become a monkey at once,
full of teasing tricks;
if something had vexed you,
I'd clown around for you.
If I could only become a monkey at once,
full of teasing tricks.

If I could only be kind as a sheep,
courageous as a lion;
if I could only have eyes like a lynx's
and slyness like a fox's.
If I could only be kind as a sheep,
courageous as a lion.

Was alles ich wär,
Das gönnt ich dir sehr;
Mit fürstlichen Gaben,
Du solltest mich haben.
Was alles ich wär,
Das gönnt ich dir sehr.

Doch bin ich, wie ich bin,
Und nimm mich nur hin!
Willst du Beßre besitzen,
So laß dir sie schnitzen.
Ich bin nun, wie ich bin;
So nimm mich nur hin!

## Wandrers Nachtlied [Ein Gleiches]

Über allen Gipfeln
Ist Ruh,
In allen Wipfeln
Spürest du
Kaum einen Hauch;
Die Vögelein schweigen im Walde.
Warte nur, balde
Ruhest du auch.

## Erlkönig

Wer reitet so spät durch Nacht und Wind?
Es ist der Vater mit seinem Kind;
Er hat den Knaben wohl in dem Arm,
Er faßt ihn sicher, er hält ihn warm.

Mein Sohn, was birgst du so bang dein Gesicht?—
Siehst, Vater, du den Erlkönig nicht?
Den Erlenkönig mit Kron und Schweif?—
Mein Sohn, es ist ein Nebelstreif.—

Whatever I would be
would be all for you;
you would have me
with princely gifts.
Whatever I would be
would be all for you.

But I am the way I am,
and just take me!
If you want to own better men,
have someone carve them for you.
I'm the way I am, that's all,
so just take me!

## Wayfarer's Night Song [Another]

Over all mountain peaks
there is rest;
in all treetops
you perceive
barely a breath;
the songbirds are silent in the forest.
Just wait, soon
you will rest too.

## Elf King

Who is riding so late through night and wind?
It is the father with his child.
He has the boy firmly in his arms,
he grasps him securely, he keeps him warm.

"My son, why are you hiding your face in such terror?"
"Father, don't you see the elf king?
The elf king with his crown and train?"
"My son, it is a patch of fog."

»Du liebes Kind, komm, geh mit mir!
Gar schöne Spiele spiel ich mit dir;
Manch bunte Blumen sind an dem Strand,
Meine Mutter hat manch gülden Gewand.«

Mein Vater, mein Vater, und hörest du nicht,
Was Erlenkönig mir leise verspricht? –
Sei ruhig, bleibe ruhig, mein Kind;
In dürren Blättern säuselt der Wind. –

»Willst, feiner Knabe, du mit mir gehn?
Meine Töchter sollen dich warten schön;
Meine Töchter führen den nächtlichen Reihn,
Und wiegen und tanzen und singen dich ein.«

Mein Vater, mein Vater, und siehst du nicht dort
Erlkönigs Töchter am düstern Ort? –
Mein Sohn, mein Sohn, ich seh es genau:
Es scheinen die alten Weiden so grau. –

»Ich liebe dich, mich reizt deine schöne Gestalt;
Und bist du nicht willig, so brauch ich Gewalt.«
Mein Vater, mein Vater, jetzt faßt er mich an!
Erlkönig hat mir ein Leids getan! –

Dem Vater grausets, er reitet geschwind,
Er hält in Armen das ächzende Kind,
Erreicht den Hof mit Müh und Not;
In seinen Armen das Kind war tot.

## Der Sänger

Was hör ich draußen vor dem Tor,
Was auf der Brücke schallen?
Laß den Gesang vor unserm Ohr
Im Saale widerhallen!
Der König sprachs, der Page lief;
Der Knabe kam, der König rief:
Laßt mir herein den Alten!

"You dear child, come along with me!
I will play really beautiful games with you;
many colorful flowers grow by the banks,
my mother has many a golden garment."

"My father, my father, and don't you hear
what the elf king is quietly promising me?"
"Be calm, stay calm, my child:
the wind is whistling in the dry leaves."

"My fine boy, do you want to come with me?
My daughters shall attend you beautifully;
My daughters lead the round dance at night,
and will rock and dance and sing you to sleep."

"My father, my father, and don't you see there
the elf king's daughters in that gloomy place?"
"My son, my son, I see it clearly:
the old willows have that gray appearance."

"I love you, your beautiful form arouses me;
and if you're not willing, I will use force."
"My father, my father, now he's seizing me!
The elf king has hurt me!"

The father is frightened, he rides swiftly,
he holds in his arms the groaning child;
he reaches his yard with effort and distress—
in his arms the child was dead.

## The Minstrel

"What do I hear outside before the gate,
what do I hear resounding on the bridge?
Let the song echo in the hall
before our ears!"
So spoke the king, the page ran out;
the boy returned, the king called:
"Let the old man in!"

Gegrüßet seid mir, edle Herrn,
Gegrüßt ihr, schöne Damen!
Welch reicher Himmel! Stern bei Stern!
Wer kennet ihre Namen?
Im Saal voll Pracht und Herrlichkeit
Schließt, Augen, euch; hier ist nicht Zeit,
Sich staunend zu ergetzen.

Der Sänger drückt' die Augen ein
Und schlug in vollen Tönen;
Die Ritter schauten mutig drein,
Und in den Schoß die Schönen.
Der König, dem das Lied gefiel,
Ließ, ihn zu ehren für sein Spiel,
Eine goldne Kette holen.

Die goldne Kette gib mir nicht,
Die Kette gib den Rittern,
Vor deren kühnem Angesicht
Der Feinde Lanzen splittern;
Gib sie dem Kanzler, den du hast,
Und laß ihn noch die goldne Last
Zu andern Lasten tragen.

Ich singe, wie der Vogel singt,
Der in den Zweigen wohnet;
Das Lied, das aus der Kehle dringt,
Ist Lohn, der reichlich lohnet.
Doch darf ich bitten, bitt ich eins:
Laß mir den besten Becher Weins
In purem Golde reichen.

Er setzt' ihn an, er trank ihn aus:
O Trank voll süßer Labe!
O wohl dem hochbeglückten Haus,
Wo das ist kleine Gabe!
Ergehts euch wohl, so denkt an mich,
Und danket Gott so warm, als ich
Für diesen Trunk euch danke.

"Greetings to you, noble lords;
greetings to you, fair ladies!
What a rich sky! One star next to another!
Who knows your names?
In this hall full of splendor and magnificence
close, my eyes; here is no time
to delight yourself with wonder."

The minstrel shut his eyes
and played full chords on his harp;
the knights had brave expressions,
the fair ladies looked down at their laps.
The king, who liked the song,
had a golden chain brought
to honor him for his playing.

"Don't give the golden chain to me,
give the chain to the knights,
at whose bold countenance
the enemy's lances splinter;
give it to this chancellor of yours,
and let him bear this golden burden, too,
along with his other burdens.

"I sing as the birds sing
that live in the branches;
the song that pours from my throat
is a sufficiently great reward.
But if I may make a request, I ask for one thing:
let me be handed the best wine
in a goblet of pure gold."

He put it to his lips, he drained it:
"O drink full of sweet refreshment!
Oh, happy is the highly fortunate house
where this is a trivial gift!
If things go well with you, think of me
and thank God as warmly as I
thank you for this drink."

## *Harfenspieler*

Wer nie sein Brot mit Tränen aß,
Wer nie die kummervollen Nächte
Auf seinem Bette weinend saß,
Der kennt euch nicht, ihr himmlischen Mächte.

Ihr führt ins Leben uns hinein,
Ihr laßt den Armen schuldig werden,
Dann überlaßt ihr ihn der Pein:
Denn alle Schuld rächt sich auf Erden.

## *Das Göttliche*

Edel sei der Mensch,
Hilfreich und gut!
Denn das allein
Unterscheidet ihn
Von allen Wesen,
Die wir kennen.

Heil den unbekannten
Höhern Wesen,
Die wir ahnen!
Ihnen gleiche der Mensch;
Sein Beispiel lehr uns
Jene glauben.

Denn unfühlend
Ist die Natur:
Es leuchtet die Sonne
Über Bös' und Gute,
Und dem Verbrecher
Glänzen wie dem Besten
Der Mond und die Sterne.

Wind und Ströme,
Donner und Hagel
Rauschen ihren Weg

## *Harpist*

The man who never ate his bread with tears,
who never sat weeping on his bed
through the sorrowful nights,
does not know you, heavenly powers.

You lead us into life,
you let a poor man acquire guilt,
then you abandon him to his pain:
for all guilt is avenged here on earth.

## *The Divine Principle*

Let man be noble,
helpful and kind!
For that alone
distinguishes him
from all other beings
that we know.

Hail the unknown
higher beings
whom we merely sense!
Let man be like them;
let his example teach us
to believe in them.

For nature
is unfeeling:
the sun shines
for evil and good men alike,
and the moon and stars beam
for the criminal
just as for the best of men.

Wind and streams,
thunder and hail
roar along their way

Und ergreifen
Vorüber eilend
Einen um den andern.

Auch so das Glück
Tappt unter die Menge,
Faßt bald des Knaben
Lockige Unschuld,
Bald auch den kahlen
Schuldigen Scheitel.

Nach ewigen, ehrnen,
Großen Gesetzen
Müssen wir alle
Unseres Daseins
Kreise vollenden.

Nur allein der Mensch
Vermag das Unmögliche:
Er unterscheidet,
Wählet und richtet;
Er kann dem Augenblick
Dauer verleihen.

Er allein darf
Den Guten lohnen,
Den Bösen strafen,
Heilen und retten,
Alles Irrende, Schweifende
Nützlich verbinden.

Und wir verehren
Die Unsterblichen,
Als wären sie Menschen,
Täten im Großen,
Was der Beste im Kleinen
Tut oder möchte.

Der edle Mensch
Sei hilfreich und gut!

and, rushing by,
seize
one man after the other.

Similarly, good fortune
gropes blindly among the multitude,
now grasping the boy's
innocent curls,
now the bald
crown of the guilty man.

In accordance with eternal, adamant,
great laws
we must
complete all the circles
of our existence.

Man alone
can do the impossible:
he makes distinctions,
choices, and judgments;
he can lend
duration to the fleeting moment.

He alone may
reward the good man,
punish the evil man,
heal and save,
tying together usefully
all that goes wandering astray.

And we honor
the immortals
as if they were human,
as if they did on a grand scale
what the best man does, or would like to,
on a small scale.

Let the noble man
be helpful and kind!

Unermüdet schaff er
Das Nützliche, Rechte,
Sei uns ein Vorbild
Jener geahneten Wesen!

## Mignon

Kennst du das Land, wo die Zitronen blühn,
Im dunkeln Laub die Gold-Orangen glühn,
Ein sanfter Wind vom blauen Himmel weht,
Die Myrte still und hoch der Lorbeer steht,
Kennst du es wohl?
                    Dahin! Dahin
Möcht ich mit dir, o mein Geliebter, ziehn!

Kennst du das Haus? Auf Säulen ruht sein Dach,
Es glänzt der Saal, es schimmert das Gemach,
Und Marmorbilder stehn und sehn mich an:
Was hat man dir, du armes Kind, getan?
Kennst du es wohl?
                    Dahin! Dahin
Möcht ich mit dir, o mein Beschützer, ziehn!

Kennst du den Berg und seinen Wolkensteg?
Das Maultier sucht im Nebel seinen Weg,
In Höhlen wohnt der Drachen alte Brut,
Es stürzt der Fels und über ihn die Flut:
Kennst du ihn wohl?
                    Dahin! Dahin
Geht unser Weg! o Vater, laß uns ziehn!

## Zueignung

Der Morgen kam; es scheuchten seine Tritte
Den leisen Schlaf, der mich gelind umfing,
Daß ich, erwacht, aus meiner stillen Hütte
Den Berg hinauf mit frischer Seele ging;

Let him tirelessly bring about
that which is useful and right,
let him be for us a prefiguration
of those beings we can only sense!

## Mignon

Do you know the land where the lemon trees blossom,
where the golden oranges glow in the dark foliage,
where a gentle breeze blows from the blue sky,
where the myrtle stands silently and the laurel grows tall,
do you know it?
                There! There
I would like to go with you, my beloved!

Do you know the house? Its roof rests on columns,
its great hall shines, its rooms glitter,
and marble statues stand looking at me:
"What have they done to you, poor child?"
Do you know it?
                There! There
I would like to go with you, my protector!

Do you know the mountain and its footbridge amid the clouds?
The mule seeks its way in the mist;
in caves the ancient brood of the dragons dwells;
the crag plummets and, over it, the waters:
do you know it?
                There! there
our path leads! O Father, let us go!

## Dedication

Morning came; its footsteps scared away
the light sleep that gently embraced me,
so that, awake, I left my silent cabin
and ascended the hill with my soul restored;

Ich freute mich bei einem jeden Schritte
Der neuen Blume, die voll Tropfen hing;
Der junge Tag erhob sich mit Entzücken,
Und alles war erquickt, mich zu erquicken.

Und wie ich stieg, zog von dem Fluß der Wiesen
Ein Nebel sich in Streifen sacht hervor;
Er wich und wechselte, mich zu umfließen,
Und wuchs geflügelt mir ums Haupt empor:
Des schönen Blicks sollt ich nicht mehr genießen,
Die Gegend deckte mir ein trüber Flor;
Bald sah ich mich von Wolken wie umgossen
Und mit mir selbst in Dämmrung eingeschlossen.

Auf einmal schien die Sonne durchzudringen,
Im Nebel ließ sich eine Klarheit sehn.
Hier sank er, leise sich hinabzuschwingen,
Hier teilt' er steigend sich um Wald und Höhn.
Wie hofft ich ihr den ersten Gruß zu bringen!
Sie hofft ich nach der Trübe doppelt schön.
Der luftge Kampf war lange nicht vollendet,
Ein Glanz umgab mich, und ich stand geblendet.

Bald machte mich, die Augen aufzuschlagen,
Ein innrer Trieb des Herzens wieder kühn,
Ich konnt es nur mit schnellen Blicken wagen,
Denn alles schien zu brennen und zu glühn.
Da schwebte, mit den Wolken hergetragen,
Ein göttlich Weib vor meinen Augen hin,
Kein schöner Bild sah ich in meinem Leben,
Sie sah mich an und blieb verweilend schweben.

Kennst du mich nicht? sprach sie mit einem Munde
Dem aller Lieb und Treue Ton entfloß:
Erkennst du mich, die ich in manche Wunde
Des Lebens dir den reinsten Balsam goß?
Du kennst mich wohl, an die, zu ewgem Bunde,
Dein strebend Herz sich fest und fester schloß.
Sah ich dich nicht mit heißen Herzenstränen
Als Knabe schon nach mir dich eifrig sehnen?

at each step I rejoiced
in the new flowers, which hung full of dewdrops;
the young day rose with delight,
and everything was refreshed, to refresh me.

And as I climbed, from the river in the meadows
a mist rose gently in patches;
it yielded and changed shape, flowing around me,
and grew, as if winged, around and over my head:
I was no longer to enjoy the beautiful view;
a dismal veil shut out the region from my eyes;
soon I found myself practically swimming in clouds
and confined in twilight with myself alone.

All at once the sun seemed to penetrate it,
a brightness could be seen through the mist.
Here it descended, winging its way gently downward;
here, rising, it distributed itself over the forest and the heights.
How I hoped to bring the sun the first greetings!
I hoped that after the dimness it would be twice as beautiful.
Before this atmospheric battle was long over,
a glow surrounded me, and I stood there dazzled.

Soon an inner compulsion of the heart once more
emboldened me to open my eyes;
I could only venture to do so with rapid glances,
because everything seemed to burn and glow.
Then, borne toward me with the clouds,
a divine woman hovered before my eyes;
I never saw a lovelier image in my life;
she looked at me and remained hovering there.

"Don't you know me?" she asked with lips
that uttered the sound of all love and faithfulness:
"Do you recognize me, I who into many a wound
poured the purest balm of life for you?
You surely know me, I to whom, in eternal alliance,
your striving heart bound itself more and more firmly.
Didn't I see you, still a boy,
eagerly yearning for me with hot tears from the heart?"

Ja! rief ich aus, indem ich selig nieder
Zur Erde sank, lang hab ich dich gefühlt;
Du gabst mir Ruh, wenn durch die jungen Glieder
Die Leidenschaft sich rastlos durchgewühlt;
Du hast mir wie mit himmlischem Gefieder
Am heißen Tag die Stirne sanft gekühlt;
Du schenktest mir der Erde beste Gaben,
Und jedes Glück will ich durch dich nur haben!

Dich nenn ich nicht. Zwar hör ich dich von vielen
Gar oft genannt, und jeder heißt dich *sein*,
Ein jedes Auge glaubt auf dich zu zielen,
Fast jedem Auge wird dein Strahl zur Pein.
Ach, da ich irrte, hatt ich viel Gespielen,
Da ich dich kenne, bin ich fast allein;
Ich muß mein Glück nur mit mir selbst genießen,
Dein holdes Licht verdecken und verschließen.

Sie lächelte, sie sprach: Du siehst, wie klug,
Wie nötig wars, euch wenig zu enthüllen!
Kaum bist du sicher vor dem gröbsten Trug,
Kaum bist du Herr vom ersten Kinderwillen,
So glaubst du dich schon Übermensch genug,
Versäumst die Pflicht des Mannes zu erfüllen!
Wieviel bist du von andern unterschieden?
Erkenne dich, leb mit der Welt in Frieden!

Verzeih mir, rief ich aus, ich meint es gut;
Soll ich umsonst die Augen offen haben?
Ein froher Wille lebt in meinem Blut,
Ich kenne ganz den Wert von deinen Gaben!
Für andre wächst in mir das edle Gut,
Ich kann und will das Pfund nicht mehr vergraben!
Warum sucht ich den Weg so sehnsuchtsvoll,
Wenn ich ihn nicht den Brüdern zeigen soll?

Und wie ich sprach, sah mich das hohe Wesen
Mit einem Blick mitleidger Nachsicht an;
Ich konnte mich in ihrem Auge lesen,
Was ich verfehlt und was ich recht getan.

"Yes!" I exclaimed, as I blissfully sank
down to the ground, "I have long felt your presence;
you gave me repose when my young limbs
were tirelessly ravaged by passion;
as if with heavenly wings, you
gently cooled my brow in the heat of day;
you gave me the earth's best gifts,
and it is only through you that I wish to gain every happiness!

"I do not name you. To be sure, I very often hear you named
by many people, and each one of them calls you 'his';
all eyes believe they are directed toward you,
but for almost all eyes your rays become a torment.
Ah, when I went astray I had many companions,
now that I know you I am nearly alone;
I must enjoy my happiness with myself only,
I must cover up and lock away your lovely light."

She smiled, she said: "You see how wise,
how necessary it was to reveal only a little to you!
While scarcely safe from the most flagrant deception,
while scarcely the master of your earliest childish desires,
you already believe you are a sufficiently superior man,
and you neglect the fulfillment of a man's duties!
How different are you from others?
Recognize yourself, live at peace with the world!"

"Forgive me," I exclaimed, "I meant well;
are my eyes open for nothing, then?
A cheerful will is coursing in my veins,
I know the full value of your gifts!
The noble possessions are growing within me for the good of others,
I can and will no longer bury my talent!
Why did I seek the path so longingly
if I am not to show it to my brothers?"

And as I spoke, the lofty being gazed at me
with a look of sympathetic indulgence;
in her eyes I could read my own self,
where I had gone wrong and what I had done right.

Sie lächelte, da war ich schon genesen,
Zu neuen Freuden stieg mein Geist heran;
Ich konnte nun mit innigem Vertrauen
Mich zu ihr nahn und ihre Nähe schauen.

Da reckte sie die Hand aus in die Streifen
Der leichten Wolken und des Dufts umher;
Wie sie ihn faßte, ließ er sich ergreifen,
Er ließ sich ziehn, es war kein Nebel mehr.
Mein Auge konnt im Tale wieder schweifen,
Gen Himmel blickt ich, er war hell und hehr.
Nur sah ich sie den reinsten Schleier halten,
Er floß um sie und schwoll in tausend Falten.

Ich kenne dich, ich kenne deine Schwächen,
Ich weiß, was Gutes in dir lebt und glimmt!
– So sagte sie, ich hör sie ewig sprechen, –
Empfange hier, was ich dir lang bestimmt!
Dem Glücklichen kann es an nichts gebrechen,
Der dies Geschenk mit stiller Seele nimmt:
Aus Morgenduft gewebt und Sonnenklarheit,
Der Dichtung Schleier aus der Hand der Wahrheit.

Und wenn es dir und deinen Freunden schwüle
Am Mittag wird, so wirf ihn in die Luft!
Sogleich umsäuselt Abendwindes Kühle,
Umhaucht euch Blumen-Würzgeruch und Duft.
Es schweigt das Wehen banger Erdgefühle,
Zum Wolkenbette wandelt sich die Gruft,
Besänftiget wird jede Lebenswelle,
Der Tag wird lieblich, und die Nacht wird helle.

So kommt denn, Freunde, wenn auf euren Wegen
Des Lebens Bürde schwer und schwerer drückt,
Wenn eure Bahn ein frischerneuter Segen
Mit Blumen ziert, mit goldnen Früchten schmückt,
Wir gehn vereint dem nächsten Tag entgegen!
So leben wir, so wandeln wir beglückt.
Und dann auch soll, wenn Enkel um uns trauern,
Zu ihrer Lust noch unsre Liebe dauern.

She smiled, and I was already cured;
My spirit rose upward toward new joys;
now with ardent confidence I was able
to approach her and take a close look at her.

Then she stretched her hand out into the patches
of light clouds and haze around us;
as she grasped at the haze, it let itself be seized,
it let itself be pulled away, it was a mist no more.
My eyes could once more roam in the valley;
I looked up at the sky, it was bright and lofty.
I only saw her hold the thinnest veil,
floating around her and billowing into a thousand folds.

"I know you, I know your weaknesses;
I know what good lives and glimmers within you!"
Thus she spoke, I hear her eternally speaking:
"Receive here what I have long intended for you!
Nothing can be lacking to the fortunate man
who takes this gift with a tranquil soul:
woven from morning haze and the sun's brightness,
the veil of poetry from the hands of Truth.

"And when you and your friends are uncomfortably warm
at midday, toss it into the air!
At once the coolness of the evening breeze will rustle about you,
and the spicy smell and fragrance of flowers will breathe around you.
The blasts of fearful earthly emotions will fall silent,
the grave will be transformed into a bed of cloud,
all the rough waves of life will be stilled,
the day will become lovely, and the night will become bright."

So come, then, friends, when on your paths
life's burden weighs more and more heavily upon you;
when a freshly renewed blessing adorns your road
with flowers and enlivens it with golden fruit,
we shall go united to meet the coming day!
Thus we shall live and walk in happiness.
And then, too, when our grandchildren mourn for us,
our love will still last for their pleasure.

## Anakreons Grab

Wo die Rose hier blüht, wo Reben um Lorbeer sich schlingen,
   Wo das Turtelchen lockt, wo sich das Grillchen ergetzt,
Welch ein Grab ist hier, das alle Götter mit Leben
   Schön bepflanzt und geziert? Es ist Anakreons Ruh.
Frühling, Sommer und Herbst genoß der glückliche Dichter;
   Vor dem Winter hat ihn endlich der Hügel geschützt.

## Mignon

Nur wer die Sehnsucht kennt,
Weiß, was ich leide!
Allein und abgetrennt
Von aller Freude,
Seh ich ans Firmament
Nach jener Seite.
Ach! der mich liebt und kennt,
Ist in der Weite.
Es schwindelt mir, es brennt
Mein Eingeweide.
Nur wer die Sehnsucht kennt,
Weiß, was ich leide!

## Cophtisches Lied

Lasset Gelehrte sich zanken und streiten,
Streng und bedächtig die Lehrer auch sein!
Alle die Weisesten aller der Zeiten
Lächeln und winken und stimmen mit ein:
Töricht, auf Beßrung der Toren zu harren!
Kinder der Klugheit, o habet die Narren
Eben zum Narren auch, wie sichs gehört!

Merlin der Alte, im leuchtenden Grabe,
Wo ich als Jüngling gesprochen ihn habe,
Hat mich mit ähnlicher Antwort belehrt:

## Anacreon's Grave

Where the rose blooms here, where vines twine around laurel,
    where the turtle-dove calls, where the cricket makes merry,
what sort of grave is this that all gods have beautifully planted
    and adorned with life? It is Anacreon's resting place.
The fortunate poet enjoyed spring, summer, and autumn;
    finally this mound has protected him from winter.

## Mignon

Only one familiar with yearning
knows what I suffer!
Alone and sundered
from all joy,
I look up at the sky
seeking the world beyond.
Ah, the man who loves me and knows me
is far away.
I'm dizzy, my heart
is burning.
Only one familiar with yearning
knows what I suffer!

## Song of the Great Cophta

Let scholars quarrel and squabble,
let teachers be severe and circumspect, too!
All the wisest men of all times
smile and nod and agree:
"Foolish to expect fools to improve!
Children of intelligence, just make fun
of fools, as is proper!"

Ancient Merlin, in his shining grave,
where I conversed with him when I was a young man,
instructed me with a similar reply:

Töricht, auf Beßrung der Toren zu harren!
Kinder der Klugheit, o habet die Narren
Eben zum Narren auch, wie sichs gehört!

Und auf den Höhen der indischen Lüfte
Und in den Tiefen ägyptischer Grüfte
Hab ich das heilige Wort nur gehört:
Töricht, auf Beßrung der Toren zu harren!
Kinder der Klugheit, o habet die Narren
Eben zum Narren auch, wie sichs gehört!

## Ein andres [Cophtisches Lied II]

Geh! gehorche meinen Winken,
Nutze deine jungen Tage,
Lerne zeitig klüger sein:
Auf des Glückes großer Wage
Steht die Zunge selten ein;
Du mußt steigen oder sinken,
Du mußt herrschen und gewinnen,
Oder dienen und verlieren,
Leiden oder triumphieren,
Amboß oder Hammer sein.

## Amor als Landschaftsmaler

Saß ich früh auf einer Felsenspitze,
Sah mit starren Augen in den Nebel;
Wie ein grau grundiertes Tuch gespannet,
Deckt' er alles in die Breit und Höhe.

Stellt' ein Knabe sich mir an die Seite,
Sagte: Lieber Freund, wie magst du starrend
Auf das leere Tuch gelassen schauen?
Hast du denn zum Malen und zum Bilden
Alle Lust auf ewig wohl verloren?

Sah ich an das Kind und dachte heimlich:
Will das Bübchen doch den Meister machen!

"Foolish to expect fools to improve!
Children of intelligence, just make fun
of fools, as is proper!"

And on the heights in the skies of India,
and in the depths of Egyptian tombs
I heard these sacred words only:
"Foolish to expect fools to improve!
Children of intelligence, just make fun
of fools, as is proper!"

## Another [Song of the Great Cophta II]

Go! obey my commands,
make use of your youth,
learn early to be wiser:
on the great scales of happiness
the pointer is seldom in repose;
you must rise or fall,
you must be a master and win
or else be a servant and lose,
suffer or triumph,
be the anvil or the hammer.

## Cupid as Landscape Painter

Early in the day I was sitting on a pointed rock,
looking into the mist with rigid eyes;
stretched out like a canvas with a gray priming,
it covered everything alongside and above.

A boy came up beside me,
and said: "My dear friend, how can you calmly
stare at that empty canvas?
Have you, then, forever lost all pleasure
in painting and creating pictures?"

I looked at the child and thought to myself:
"This little boy wants to play the master painter!"

Willst du immer trüb und müßig bleiben,
Sprach der Knabe, kann nichts Kluges werden;
Sieh, ich will dir gleich ein Bildchen malen,
Dich ein hübsches Bildchen malen lehren.

Und er richtete den Zeigefinger,
Der so rötlich war wie eine Rose,
Nach dem weiten ausgespannten Teppich,
Fing mit seinem Finger an zu zeichnen.

Oben malt' er eine schöne Sonne,
Die mir in die Augen mächtig glänzte,
Und den Saum der Wolken macht' er golden,
Ließ die Strahlen durch die Wolken dringen;
Malte dann die zarten leichten Wipfel
Frisch erquickter Bäume, zog die Hügel,
Einen nach dem andern, frei dahinter;
Unten ließ ers nicht an Wasser fehlen,
Zeichnete den Fluß so ganz natürlich,
Daß er schien im Sonnenstrahl zu glitzern,
Daß er schien am hohen Rand zu rauschen.

Ach, da standen Blumen an dem Flusse,
Und da waren Farben auf der Wiese,
Gold und Schmelz und Purpur und ein Grünes,
Alles wie Smaragd und wie Karfunkel!
Hell und rein lasiert' er drauf den Himmel
Und die blauen Berge fern und ferner,
Daß ich, ganz entzückt und neugeboren,
Bald den Maler, bald das Bild beschaute.

Hab ich doch, so sagt' er dir bewiesen,
Daß ich dieses Handwerk gut verstehe;
Doch es ist das Schwerste noch zurücke.

Zeichnete darnach mit spitzem Finger
Und mit großer Sorgfalt an dem Wäldchen,
Grad ans Ende, wo die Sonne kräftig
Von dem hellen Boden widerglänzte,
Zeichnete das allerliebste Mädchen,
Wohlgebildet, zierlich angekleidet,

"If you intend to remain always gloomy and idle,"
said the boy, "nothing decent can come of it;
look, I'll paint you a little picture right now,
I'll teach you how to paint a pretty little picture."

And he extended his index finger,
which was as pink as a rose,
toward the broadly outstretched cloth,
and began to draw with his finger.

On top he painted a beautiful sun
that shone strongly into my eyes,
and he made the edges of the clouds golden,
allowing the beams to pierce through the clouds;
then he painted the gentle, light tops
of newly refreshed trees, drew in the hills
freely behind them, one after the other;
at the bottom he didn't let the picture lack for water,
but drew in the river so very naturally
that it seemed to glisten in the sunbeams,
that it seemed to rush past its tall banks.

Ah, there stood flowers by the river,
and there were colors on the meadow,
gold and enamel and purple and a shade of green,
all like emeralds and garnets!
Brightly and cleanly he added a glaze over the sky
and the blue mountains receding into the distance,
so that, completely delighted and born anew,
I looked now at the painter, now at the picture.

"So," he said, "I have really proved to you
that I understand this craft well;
but the hardest part is still to come."

Thereupon, with the tip of his finger
and with the greatest care, he drew, by the little patch of woods,
right where it ended, where the sun was powerfully
reflected off the bright ground,
he drew the loveliest of all girls,
well shaped, prettily dressed,

Frische Wangen unter braunen Haaren,
Und die Wangen waren von der Farbe
Wie das Fingerchen, das sie gebildet.

O du Knabe! rief ich, welch ein Meister
Hat in seine Schule dich genommen,
Daß du so geschwind und so natürlich
Alles klug beginnst und gut vollendest?

Da ich noch so rede, sieh, da rühret
Sich ein Windchen und bewegt die Gipfel,
Kräuselt alle Wellen auf dem Flusse,
Füllt den Schleier des vollkommnen Mädchens
Und, was mich Erstaunten mehr erstaunte,
Fängt das Mädchen an, den Fuß zu rühren,
Geht zu kommen, nähert sich dem Orte,
Wo ich mit dem losen Lehrer sitze.

Da nun alles, alles sich bewegte,
Bäume, Fluß und Blumen und der Schleier
Und der zarte Fuß der Allerschönsten,
Glaubt ihr wohl, ich sei auf meinem Felsen
Wie ein Felsen still und fest geblieben?

## Römische Elegie I

Saget, Steine, mir an, o sprecht, ihr hohen Paläste!
    Straßen, redet ein Wort! Genius, regst du dich nicht?
Ja, es ist alles beseelt in deinen heiligen Mauern,
    Ewige Roma; nur mir schweiget noch alles so still.
O wer flüstert mir zu, an welchem Fenster erblick ich
    Einst das holde Geschöpf, das mich versengend erquickt?
Ahn ich die Wege noch nicht, durch die ich immer und immer,
    Zu ihr und von ihr zu gehn, opfre die köstliche Zeit?
Noch betracht ich Kirch und Palast, Ruinen und Säulen,
    Wie ein bedächtiger Mann schicklich die Reise benutzt.
Doch bald ist es vorbei; dann wird ein einziger Tempel,
    Amors Tempel, nur sein, der den Geweihten empfängt.
Eine Welt zwar bist du, o Rom; doch ohne die Liebe
    Wäre die Welt nicht die Welt, wäre denn Rom auch nicht Rom.

rosy cheeks below brown hair,
and the cheeks were the same color
as the little finger that drew them.

"My boy!" I shouted. "What master
accepted you in his school,
for you so quickly and so naturally
to begin everything wisely and end it well?"

While I was still saying that, behold, a breeze
arises and stirs the mountaintops,
crinkles all the waves in the river,
puffs up the veil of that perfect girl
and, what astonished me more, though already astonished,
the girl begins to move her feet,
starts walking, and approaches the spot
where I am sitting with my impudent teacher.

Now that everything, everything was in motion,
trees, river, and flowers, and the veil
and delicate feet of that wondrous beauty,
do you really think I remained on my rock
quiet and motionless as a rock?

## Roman Elegy I

Stones, announce me! Speak, you lofty palaces!
　　Streets, say just a word! Genius of the place, won't you bestir yourself?
Yes, everything within your sacred walls is animated with life,
　　eternal Rome; only for me everything is still so silent.
Oh, who will whisper to me, at what window will I catch sight
　　of the lovely creature who will sear me into new life?
Do I not yet foresee the paths by which, again and again,
　　I will sacrifice my precious time going to her and from her?
I am still contemplating churches and palaces, ruins and columns,
　　the way a prudent man makes proper use of his travels.
But soon that will be over, and then it will be one temple alone,
　　Love's temple, that receives its initiate.
To be sure, you're a world, Rome, but without love
　　the world wouldn't be the world, nor would Rome be Rome.

## Römische Elegie III

Laß dich, Geliebte, nicht reun, daß du mir so schnell dich ergeben!
  Glaub es, ich denke nicht frech, denke nicht niedrig von dir.
Vielfach wirken die Pfeile des Amor: einige ritzen,
  Und vom schleichenden Gift kranket auf Jahre das Herz.
Aber mächtig befiedert, mit frisch geschliffener Schärfe
  Dringen die andern ins Mark, zünden behende das Blut.
In der heroischen Zeit, da Götter und Göttinnen liebten,
  Folgte Begierde dem Blick, folgte Genuß der Begier.
Glaubst du, es habe sich lange die Göttin der Liebe besonnen,
  Als im Idäischen Hain einst ihr Anchises gefiel?
Hätte Luna gesäumt, den schönen Schläfer zu küssen,
  O, so hätt ihn geschwind, neidend, Aurora geweckt.
Hero erblickte Leandern am lauten Fest, und behende
  Stürzte der Liebende sich heiß in die nächtliche Flut.
Rhea Sylvia wandelt, die fürstliche Jungfrau, der Tiber
  Wasser zu schöpfen, hinab, und sie ergreifet der Gott.
So erzeugte die Söhne sich Mars! – Die Zwillinge tränket
  Eine Wölfin, und Rom nennt sich die Fürstin der Welt.

## Römische Elegie IV

Fromm sind wir Liebende, still verehren wir alle Dämonen,
  Wünschen uns jeglichen Gott, jegliche Göttin geneigt.
Und so gleichen wir euch, o römische Sieger! Den Göttern
  Aller Völker der Welt bietet ihr Wohnungen an,
Habe sie schwarz und streng aus altem Basalt der Ägypter,
  Oder ein Grieche sie weiß, reizend, aus Marmor geformt.
Doch verdrießet es nicht die Ewigen, wenn wir besonders
  Weihrauch köstlicher Art Einer der Göttlichen streun.
Ja, wir bekennen euch gern: es bleiben unsre Gebete,
  Unser täglicher Dienst Einer Besonders geweiht.
Schalkhaft, munter und ernst begehen wir heimliche Feste,
  Und das Schweigen geziemt allen Geweihten genau.
Eh an die Ferse lockten wir selbst durch gräßliche Taten
  Uns die Erinnyen her, wagten es eher, des Zeus
Hartes Gericht am rollenden Rad und am Felsen zu dulden,
  Als dem reizenden Dienst unser Gemüt zu entziehn.

## Roman Elegy III

Let it be no cause for regret, darling, that you yielded to me so quickly!
  Believe me, I have no insolent thoughts, no low thoughts, about you.
Cupid's arrows have varying effects: some of them scratch a person,
  and his heart is ill for years with the creeping poison.
But others, strongly feathered, with freshly sharpened points,
  penetrate to the marrow and inflame the blood rapidly.
In the heroic age, when gods and goddesses loved,
  desire followed directly on first sight, and enjoyment directly on desire.
Do you believe that the goddess of love stopped to think it over a long time
  when Anchises pleased her long ago in the grove of Mount Ida?
If the moon goddess had hesitated to kiss the handsome sleeper,
  then envious Aurora would have awakened him swiftly.
Hero caught sight of Leander at the noisy feast, and rapidly
  the lover plunged hotly into the waters at night.
Rhea Sylvia, a royal maiden, goes down to draw water
  from the Tiber and is seized by the god.
Thus Mars begat the sons for himself!—The twins were nursed
  by a she-wolf, and Rome calls itself queen of the world.

## Roman Elegy IV

We lovers are pious, we quietly revere all deities,
  wishing every god and every goddess to be favorably inclined toward us.
And in that way we are like you, Roman victors! To the gods
  of all nations in the world you offer dwelling places,
whether an Egyptian shaped them, black and austere, out of old basalt,
  or a Greek out of marble, white and charming.
But it doesn't vex the Eternal Ones if we scatter incense
  of a specially precious kind before a single one among the goddesses.
Yes, we gladly confess it to you all: our prayers,
  our daily service, is always consecrated to one goddess in particular.
Roguishly, briskly, and earnestly we celebrate secret feasts,
  and silence befits all initiates perfectly.
Sooner would we lure the Furies to dog our heels
  because of our horrible deeds; sooner would we venture to undergo
Zeus's severe judgment on the rolling wheel and on the crag,
  than to withdraw our mind from that charming service.

Diese Göttin, sie heißt *Gelegenheit,* lernet sie kennen!
Sie erscheinet euch oft, immer in andrer Gestalt.
Tochter des Proteus möchte sie sein, mit Thetis gezeuget,
Deren verwandelte List manchen Heroen betrog.
So betriegt nun die Tochter den Unerfahrnen, den Blöden:
Schlummernde necket sie stets, Wachende fliegt sie vorbei;
Gern ergibt sie sich nur dem raschen, tätigen Manne:
Dieser findet sie zahm, spielend und zärtlich und hold.
Einst erschien sie auch mir, ein bräunliches Mädchen, die Haare
Fielen ihr dunkel und reich über die Stirne herab,
Kurze Locken ringelten sich ums zierliche Hälschen,
Ungeflochtenes Haar krauste vom Scheitel sich auf.
Und ich verkannte sie nicht, ergriff die Eilende, lieblich
Gab sie Umarmung und Kuß bald mir gelehrig zurück.
O wie war ich beglückt! – Doch stille, die Zeit ist vorüber,
Und umwunden bin ich, römische Flechten, von euch.

## Römische Elegie V

Froh empfind ich mich nun auf klassischem Boden begeistert;
Vor- und Mitwelt spricht lauter und reizender mir.
Hier befolg ich den Rat, durchblättre die Werke der Alten
Mit geschäftiger Hand, täglich mit neuem Genuß.
Aber die Nächte hindurch hält Amor mich anders beschäftigt;
Werd ich auch halb nur gelehrt, bin ich doch doppelt beglückt.
Und belehr ich mich nicht, indem ich des lieblichen Busens
Formen spähe, die Hand leite die Hüften hinab?
Dann versteh ich den Marmor erst recht; ich denk und vergleiche,
Sehe mit fühlendem Aug, fühle mit sehender Hand.
Raubt die Liebste denn gleich mir einige Stunden des Tages,
Gibt sie Stunden der Nacht mir zur Entschädigung hin.
Wird doch nicht immer geküßt, es wird vernünftig gesprochen;
Überfällt sie der Schlaf, lieg ich und denke mir viel.
Oftmals hab ich auch schon in ihren Armen gedichtet
Und des Hexameters Maß leise mit fingernder Hand
Ihr auf den Rücken gezählt. Sie atmet in lieblichem Schlummer,
Und es durchglühet ihr Hauch mir bis ins Tiefste die Brust.
Amor schüret die Lamp indes und denket der Zeiten,
Da er den nämlichen Dienst seinen Triumvirn getan.

This goddess is called Opportunity; get to know her!
  She appears to you often, always in a different shape.
She might be a daughter of Proteus, engendered along with Thetis,
  whose cunning in transformations deceived many a hero.
Thus that daughter now deceives the inexperienced or simple man:
  she constantly teases those who slumber, and flies away from those who are awake.
She yields gladly only to the quick, active man:
  Such a man finds her tame and playful, delicate and loving.
Once she appeared to me, too, as a brunette girl; her hair
  fell down, dark and abundant, onto her forehead;
short curls spiraled around her pretty little neck;
  unbraided hair curled up from the crown of her head.
And I didn't fail to recognize her, I seized her as she hastened past; lovingly
  she soon returned my embrace and kiss, a quick learner.
Oh, how happy I was!—But quiet, that time has gone by,
  and I am enlaced round about with you, Roman braids.

## Roman Elegy V

I now find myself cheerfully inspired on Classic soil;
  the past and present worlds speak to me more clearly and charmingly.
Here I follow the advice and leaf through the works of the ancients
  with a busy hand, with new enjoyment every day.
But all through the nights Cupid keeps me busy at other things;
  even though I get only half educated, I am twice as happy.
And isn't it educational to spy out the forms
  of a lovely bosom, to let my hands glide down hips?
It's then that I begin to understand marble statues; I think and compare;
  I see with a feeling eye, feel with a seeing hand.
Although my sweetheart steals a few hours of my day,
  she gives me hours of the night in compensation.
We aren't always kissing, either; we have sensible conversations;
  if sleep overcomes her, I lie there and think a lot.
Often, so far, I have composed poetry in her arms,
  and with gently tapping fingers I have counted out
the hexameter's meter on her back. She breathes in lovely slumber,
  and her breath warms me to the bottom of my heart.
Meanwhile Cupid pokes up the lamp, recalling the times
  when he performed the same service for his triumvirs.

## Römische Elegie XVI

»Warum bist du, Geliebter, nicht heute zur Vigne gekommen?
   Einsam, wie ich versprach, wartet ich oben auf dich.«–
Beste, schon war ich hinein; da sah ich zum Glücke den Oheim
   Neben den Stöcken, bemüht, hin sich und her sich zu drehn.
Schleichend eilt ich hinaus!–»O welch ein Irrtum ergriff dich!
   Eine Scheuche nur wars, was dich vertrieb! Die Gestalt
Flickten wir emsig zusammen aus alten Kleidern und Rohren;
   Emsig half ich daran, selbst mir zu schaden bemüht.«–
Nun, des Alten Wunsch ist erfüllt; den losesten Vogel
   Scheucht' er heute, der ihm Gärtchen und Nichte bestiehlt.

## Der Rattenfänger

Ich bin der wohlbekannte Sänger,
Der vielgereiste Rattenfänger,
Den diese altberühmte Stadt
Gewiß besonders nötig hat.
Und wärens Ratten noch so viele,
Und wären Wiesel mit im Spiele,
Von allen säubr ich diesen Ort,
Sie müssen miteinander fort.

Dann ist der gut gelaunte Sänger
Mitunter auch ein Kinderfänger,
Der selbst die wildesten bezwingt,
Wenn er die goldnen Märchen singt.
Und wären Knaben noch so trutzig,
Und wären Mädchen noch so stutzig,
In meine Saiten greif ich ein,
Sie müssen alle hinterdrein.

Dann ist der vielgewandte Sänger
Gelegentlich ein Mädchenfänger;
In keinem Städtchen langt er an,
Wo ers nicht mancher angetan.
Und wären Mädchen noch so blöde,
Und wären Weiber noch so spröde,

## Roman Elegy XVI

"Darling, why didn't you come today to the house in the vineyard?
  I was waiting up there alone for you, as I had promised."
"Dear, I was already there when I luckily saw your uncle
  next to the vinestocks, busy turning back and forth.
I sneaked out in a hurry!" "Oh, what a mistake you made!
  It was only a scarecrow that chased you away! We busily
pieced the figure together out of old clothes and reeds;
  I helped busily, working for my own disadvantage."
"Well, the old man's wish came true; today he scared away
  the most wanton bird, who robs his garden and steals his niece."

## The Ratcatcher

I am the well-known singer,
the widely traveled ratcatcher,
whom this long-famous city
definitely has a special need for.
And no matter how numerous the rats are,
and even if weasels are involved,
I'll cleanse this place of them all,
each and every one has got to go.

And then, this good-tempered singer
is sometimes also a child catcher,
and can subdue even the wildest ones
when he sings his golden tales.
And no matter how defiant the boys are,
and how recalcitrant the girls are,
I play a chord on my strings
and they all have to follow me.

And then the very resourceful singer
is occasionally a girl catcher;
he never arrives in any town
without turning the head of many a one.
And no matter how bashful the girls are,
and how standoffish the women are,

Doch allen wird so liebebang
Bei Zaubersaiten und Gesang.
(Von Anfang)

## *Die Spinnerin*

Als ich still und ruhig spann,
Ohne nur zu stocken,
Trat ein schöner junger Mann
Nahe mir zum Rocken.

Lobte, was zu loben war,
Sollte das was schaden?
Mein dem Flachse gleiches Haar,
Und den gleichen Faden.

Ruhig war er nicht dabei,
Ließ es nicht beim alten;
Und der Faden riß entzwei,
Den ich lang erhalten.

Und des Flachses Stein-Gewicht
Gab noch viele Zahlen;
Aber, ach, ich konnte nicht
Mehr mit ihnen prahlen.

Als ich sie zum Weber trug,
Fühlt ich was sich regen,
Und mein armes Herze schlug
Mit geschwindern Schlägen.

Nun, beim heißen Sonnenstich,
Bring ichs auf die Bleiche,
Und mit Mühe bück ich mich
Nach dem nächsten Teiche.

Was ich in dem Kämmerlein
Still und fein gesponnen,
Kommt – wie kann es anders sein? –
Endlich an die Sonnen.

they all become atremble with love
when I pluck my magic strings and sing.
(Da capo)

## The Spinner

While I was spinning quietly and peacefully,
without even pausing,
a handsome young man stepped
up to me by the distaff.

He praised what there was to praise
(could that do any harm?):
my hair that resembled flax,
and the thread of the same color.

While saying this, he didn't remain calm
or leave things as they were,
and the thread ripped
that I had long preserved.

And the heavy mass of flax
still yielded many skeins of yarn,
but alas, I could
no longer boast about them.

When I brought them to the weaver
I felt something stirring,
my poor heart pounded
with quicker beats.

Now, as the sun shines down hotly,
I bring it to the bleaching field,
and only with difficulty do I stoop down
to the nearest pond.

What I span quietly and finely
in my little bedroom,
will finally—how can it be otherwise?—
come to the light of the sun.

## Meeres Stille

Tiefe Stille herrscht im Wasser,
Ohne Regung ruht das Meer,
Und bekümmert sieht der Schiffer
Glatte Fläche ringsumher.
Keine Luft von keiner Seite!
Todesstille fürchterlich!
In der ungeheuern Weite
Reget keine Welle sich.

## Glückliche Fahrt

Die Nebel zerreißen,
Der Himmel ist helle,
Und Äolus löset
Das ängstliche Band.
Es säuseln die Winde,
Es rührt sich der Schiffer.
Geschwinde! Geschwinde!
Es teilt sich die Welle,
Es naht sich die Ferne;
Schon seh ich das Land!

## Mignon

Heiß mich nicht reden, heiß mich schweigen,
Denn mein Geheimnis ist mir Pflicht;
Ich möchte dir mein ganzes Innre zeigen,
Allein das Schicksal will es nicht.

Zur rechten Zeit vertreibt der Sonne Lauf
Die finstre Nacht, und sie muß sich erhellen;
Der harte Fels schließt seinen Busen auf,
Mißgönnt der Erde nicht die tiefverborgnen Quellen.

## Calm at Sea

Deep calm prevails on the waters,
the sea reposes without a stir,
and, in concern, the seaman
sees a smooth surface all around.
No breeze from any quarter!
a frightening, deathly calm!
In the immense expanse
no wave stirs.

## Fortunate Voyage

The mists disperse,
the sky is bright,
and Aeolus unties
the fearful knot.
The winds whistle,
the seaman bestirs himself.
Quickly! Quickly!
The waves are parting,
that which was distant draws near;
I already see land!

## Mignon

Do not bid me to speak, bid me be silent,
for keeping my secret is a duty to me;
I'd like to tell you all my inmost thoughts,
but my destiny doesn't allow me to.

When the right time comes, the sun in its course drives away
dark night, and it is compelled to grow bright;
flinty rock opens its bosom
and doesn't begrudge the earth its deeply concealed springs.

Ein jeder sucht im Arm des Freundes Ruh,
Dort kann die Brust in Klagen sich ergießen;
Allein ein Schwur drückt mir die Lippen zu,
Und nur ein Gott vermag sie aufzuschließen.

## Harfenspieler

An die Türen will ich schleichen,
Still und sittsam will ich stehn;
Fromme Hand wird Nahrung reichen,
Und ich werde weitergehn.
Jeder wird sich glücklich scheinen,
Wenn mein Bild vor ihm erscheint;
Eine Träne wird er weinen,
Und ich weiß nicht, was er weint.

## Nähe des Geliebten

Ich denke dein, wenn mir der Sonne Schimmer
        Vom Meere strahlt;
Ich denke dein, wenn sich des Mondes Flimmer
        In Quellen malt.

Ich sehe dich, wenn auf dem fernen Wege
        Der Staub sich hebt;
In tiefer Nacht, wenn auf dem schmalen Stege
        Der Wandrer bebt.

Ich höre dich, wenn dort mit dumpfem Rauschen
        Die Welle steigt.
Im stillen Haine geh ich oft zu lauschen,
        Wenn alles schweigt.

Ich bin bei dir, du seist auch noch so ferne,
        Du bist mir nah!
Die Sonne sinkt, bald leuchten mir die Sterne.
        O wärst du da!

Each man seeks repose in his friend's arms;
there his breast can pour itself out in laments;
but an oath keeps my lips closed,
and only a god is able to open them.

## Harpist

I shall steal up to people's doorways,
I shall stand quietly and demurely;
pious hands will hold out food to me,
and I shall continue on my way.
Everyone will consider himself lucky
when my image appears before him;
he will shed a tear
and I won't know what he is crying over.

## Nearness of the Loved One

I think of you when I see the sun's glimmer
          reflected from the sea;
I think of you when the moon's glitter
          is painted in the fountains.

I see you when on the distant road
          the dust rises;
late at night, when on the narrow footbridge
          the wayfarer trembles.

I hear you when, over there, with a muffled roar
          the wave surges.
I often walk in the silent grove to listen
          when all is still.

I am with you, no matter how far away you are;
          you are close to me!
The sun is setting, soon the stars will shine for me.
          If you were only here!

## *Wer kauft Liebesgötter?*

Von allen schönen Waren,
Zum Markte hergefahren,
Wird keine mehr behagen,
Als die wir euch getragen
Aus fremden Ländern bringen.
O höret, was wir singen!
Und seht die schönen Vögel,
Sie stehen zum Verkauf.

Zuerst beseht den großen,
Den lustigen, den losen!
Er hüpfet leicht und munter
Von Baum und Busch herunter;
Gleich ist er wieder droben.
Wir wollen ihn nicht loben.
O seht den muntern Vogel!
Er steht hier zum Verkauf.

Betrachtet nun den kleinen,
Er will bedächtig scheinen,
Und doch ist er der lose,
So gut als wie der große;
Er zeiget meist im stillen
Den allerbesten Willen.
Der lose kleine Vogel,
Er steht hier zum Verkauf.

O seht das kleine Täubchen,
Das liebe Turtelweibchen!
Die Mädchen sind so zierlich,
Verständig und manierlich;
Sie mag sich gerne putzen
Und eure Liebe nutzen.
Der kleine zarte Vogel,
Er steht hier zum Verkauf.

Wir wollen sie nicht loben,
Sie stehn zu allen Proben.

## Who'll Buy Cupids?

Of all the lovely merchandise
brought here to the market,
none will satisfy you more
than what we are bringing you,
imported from foreign countries.
Oh, listen to what we sing!
And look at the beautiful birds,
which are for sale.

First look at the big one,
the merry one, the wanton one!
He hops lightly and briskly
down from trees and bushes;
in a trice he's back up there.
We don't intend to praise him.
Oh, look at the lively bird!
He's for sale here.

Now observe the little one;
he tries to look sedate,
but he's as much of a madcap
as the big one;
generally, in private he exhibits
the best will in the world.
The wanton little bird
is for sale here.

Oh, look at the little dove,
the dear female turtle-dove!
Girls are so pretty,
clever and well-mannered;
she likes to dress up
and make use of your love.
The tender little bird
is for sale here.

We don't intend to praise them,
you can try them out all you want.

Sie lieben sich das Neue;
Doch über ihre Treue
Verlangt nicht Brief und Siegel,
Sie haben alle Flügel.
Wie artig sind die Vögel,
Wie reizend ist der Kauf!

## Mignon

So laßt mich scheinen, bis ich werde;
Zieht mir das weiße Kleid nicht aus!
Ich eile von der schönen Erde
Hinab in jenes feste Haus.

Dort ruh ich eine kleine Stille,
Dann öffnet sich der frische Blick,
Ich lasse dann die reine Hülle,
Den Gürtel und den Kranz zurück.

Und jene himmlischen Gestalten,
Sie fragen nicht nach Mann und Weib,
Und keine Kleider, keine Falten
Umgeben den verklärten Leib.

Zwar lebt ich ohne Sorg und Mühe,
Doch fühlt ich tiefen Schmerz genung.
Vor Kummer altert ich zu frühe –
Macht mich auf ewig wieder jung!

## Der Schatzgräber

Arm am Beutel, krank am Herzen,
Schleppt ich meine langen Tage.
Armut ist die größte Plage,
Reichtum ist das höchste Gut!

hey love novelties;
ut don't ask for stamped affidavits
s to their faithfulness;
ey all have wings.
ow cute the birds are,
ow charming it is to buy them!

## Mignon

Let me appear this way until I become real;
on't take off my white robe!
hasten from the beautiful earth
own to that secure abode.

here I shall rest for a brief, quiet time;
en my eyes, refreshed, will open;
en I shall leave behind this pure covering,
he belt and the garland.

nd those heavenly beings,
hey do not ask if you are man or woman,
nd no garments, no folds of drapery
ncircle your transfigured body.

o be sure, I lived without worry or effort,
ut I felt enough profound sorrow.
rom grief I grew old too soon—
ake me eternally young again!

## The Treasure Seeker

Poor in purse, sick at heart,
dragged out my tiresome days.
overty is the greatest plague,
vealth is the supreme good!

Und, zu enden meine Schmerzen,
Ging ich, einen Schatz zu graben.
Meine Seele sollst du haben!
Schrieb ich hin mit eignem Blut.

Und so zog ich Kreis' um Kreise,
Stellte wunderbare Flammen,
Kraut und Knochenwerk zusammen:
Die Beschwörung war vollbracht.
Und auf die gelernte Weise
Grub ich nach dem alten Schatze
Auf dem angezeigten Platze;
Schwarz und stürmisch war die Nacht.

Und ich sah ein Licht von weiten,
Und es kam gleich einem Sterne
Hinten aus der fernsten Ferne,
Eben als es Zwölfe schlug.
Und da galt kein Vorbereiten:
Heller wards mit einem Male
Von dem Glanz der vollen Schale,
Die ein schöner Knabe trug.

Holde Augen sah ich blinken
Unter dichtem Blumenkranze;
In des Trankes Himmelsglanze
Trat er in den Kreis herein.
Und er hieß mich freundlich trinken;
Und ich dacht: es kann der Knabe
Mit der schönen lichten Gabe
Wahrlich nicht der Böse sein.

Trinke Mut des reinen Lebens!
Dann verstehst du die Belehrung,
Kommst, mit ängstlicher Beschwörung,
Nicht zurück an diesen Ort.
Grabe hier nicht mehr vergebens:
Tages Arbeit! Abends Gäste!
Saure Wochen! Frohe Feste!
Sei dein künftig Zauberwort.

nd, to end my sorrows,
went out looking for buried treasure.
ou shall have my soul!"
wrote in my own blood.

nd so I drew one circle around another,
placed together wondrous flames,
erbs, and bones:
e conjuration was performed.
nd in the manner I had learned
dug for the ancient treasure
the indicated place;
e night was black and stormy.

nd far away I saw a light,
nd, like a star, it came
ut of the remote distance beyond,
st as it was striking twelve.
nd then no preparation could help:
ll at once the scene grew brighter
om the glow of the filled cup
hat a good-looking boy was carrying.

saw lovely eyes twinkling
eneath a dense garland of flowers;
n the heavenly glow of the beverage
e stepped into the circle.
nd he amiably bade me drink;
nd I thought: "This boy,
with his beautiful, bright gift,
ruly cannot be the Evil One."

Drink courage to live purely!
hen you'll understand the lesson
nd you won't return to this place
with anxious conjurations.
Dig here in vain no longer:
During the day, labor! At night, guests!
Difficult weekdays! Happy holidays!'
Let that be your magic spell in the future."

## Die Braut von Korinth

Nach Korinthus von Athen gezogen
Kam ein Jüngling, dort noch unbekannt.
Einen Bürger hofft' er sich gewogen;
Beide Väter waren gastverwandt,
Hatten frühe schon
Töchterchen und Sohn
Braut und Bräutigam voraus genannt.

Aber wird er auch willkommen scheinen,
Wenn er teuer nicht die Gunst erkauft?
Er ist noch ein Heide mit den Seinen,
Und sie sind schon Christen und getauft.
Keimt ein Glaube neu,
Wird oft Lieb und Treu
Wie ein böses Unkraut ausgerauft.

Und schon lag das ganze Haus im stillen,
Vater, Töchter, nur die Mutter wacht;
Sie empfängt den Gast mit bestem Willen,
Gleich ins Prunkgemach wird er gebracht.
Wein und Essen prangt,
Eh er es verlangt:
So versorgend wünscht sie gute Nacht.

Aber bei dem wohlbestellten Essen
Wird die Lust der Speise nicht erregt;
Müdigkeit läßt Speis und Trank vergessen,
Daß er angekleidet sich aufs Bette legt;
Und er schlummert fast,
Als ein seltner Gast
Sich zur offnen Tür herein bewegt.

Denn er sieht, bei seiner Lampe Schimmer
Tritt, mit weißem Schleier und Gewand,
Sittsam still ein Mädchen in das Zimmer,
Um die Stirn ein schwarz- und goldnes Band.
Wie sie ihn erblickt,
Hebt sie, die erschrickt,
Mit Erstaunen eine weiße Hand.

## The Bride of Corinth

Traveling to Corinth from Athens
came a young man, still unknown there.
He hoped that a townsman would look on him with favor;
the two fathers had pledged mutual hospitality,
and, much earlier, had
promised that their daughter and son
would some day be bride and groom.

But will he still seem welcome there
if he doesn't pay dearly for their good graces?
He and his family are still pagans,
while the others are already Christians and baptized.
When a new religion arises,
love and fidelity are often
torn out like an evil weed.

And the entire household was already silent,
father and daughters; only the mother is awake.
She receives the guest with great kindness;
he is brought directly into the best room.
Wine and food are served magnificently
before he even asks for them:
and, thus attending to his needs, she wishes him good night.

But at the well-arranged meal
appetite for food is not aroused;
weariness makes him forget food and drink,
so that he lies down on the bed fully clothed;
and he is nearly asleep
when a strange guest
enters through the open door.

For he sees how, in the glimmer of his lamp,
a girl with a white veil and robe
steps into the room in demure silence,
a black-and-gold band around her brow.
As she catches sight of him,
she is frightened and raises
one white hand in amazement.

Bin ich, rief sie aus, so fremd im Hause,
Daß ich von dem Gaste nichts vernahm?
Ach, so hält man mich in meiner Klause!
Und nun überfällt mich hier die Scham.
Ruhe nur so fort
Auf dem Lager dort,
Und ich gehe schnell, so wie ich kam.

Bleibe, schönes Mädchen! ruft der Knabe,
Rafft von seinem Lager sich geschwind:
Hier ist Ceres', hier ist Bacchus' Gabe,
Und du bringst den Amor, liebes Kind!
Bist vor Schrecken blaß!
Liebe, komm und laß,
Laß uns sehn, wie froh die Götter sind.

Ferne bleib, o Jüngling! bleibe stehen;
Ich gehöre nicht den Freuden an.
Schon der letzte Schritt ist, ach! geschehen
Durch der guten Mutter kranken Wahn,
Die genesend schwur:
Jugend und Natur
Sei dem Himmel künftig untertan.

Und der alten Götter bunt Gewimmel
Hat sogleich das stille Haus geleert.
Unsichtbar wird Einer nur im Himmel,
Und ein Heiland wird am Kreuz verehrt;
Opfer fallen hier,
Weder Lamm noch Stier,
Aber Menschenopfer unerhört.

Und er fragt und wäget alle Worte,
Deren keines seinem Geist entgeht.
Ist es möglich, daß am stillen Orte
Die geliebte Braut hier vor mir steht?
Sei die Meine nur!
Unsrer Väter Schwur
Hat vom Himmel Segen uns erfleht.

"Am I," she exclaimed, "such a stranger in the house
that I heard nothing about the guest?
Ah, how close they keep me in the seclusion of my cell!
And now I am covered with shame here.
Just keep resting
on your bed there,
and I'll leave quickly just as I came."

"Stay, beautiful girl!" calls the lad,
who rapidly jumps out of bed:
"Here is the gift of Ceres, here is that of Bacchus,
and you bring Love, dear child!
You're pale with fright!
Darling, come and let,
let us see how happy the gods are."

"Stay away, young man! Stay where you are;
I cannot participate in pleasure.
The final step, alas, was already taken
through my good mother's delusion when she was ill;
when she was recovering, she made a vow
that youth and nature
would henceforth be submissive to heaven.

"And the varied throng of the old gods
immediately left our house to its silence.
One person alone remains invisible in heaven,
and a Savior is revered on the Cross;
sacrificial victims are offered here,
neither lambs nor bulls,
but unheard-of human sacrifices."

And he questions her and weighs all her words,
none of which escapes his mind.
"Is it possible that here in this silent spot
my beloved bride is standing before me?
Be mine!
Our fathers' vow
has called down heaven's blessing on us."

Mich erhältst du nicht, du gute Seele!
Meiner zweiten Schwester gönnt man dich.
Wenn ich mich in stiller Klause quäle,
Ach! in ihren Armen denk an mich,
Die an dich nur denkt,
Die sich liebend kränkt;
In die Erde bald verbirgt sie sich.

Nein! bei dieser Flamme seis geschworen,
Gütig zeigt sie Hymen uns voraus;
Bist der Freude nicht und mir verloren,
Kommst mit mir in meines Vaters Haus.
Liebchen, bleibe hier!
Feire gleich mit mir
Unerwartet unsern Hochzeitschmaus.

Und schon wechseln sie der Treue Zeichen;
Golden reicht sie ihm die Kette dar,
Und er will ihr eine Schale reichen,
Silbern, künstlich, wie nicht eine war.
Die ist nicht für mich;
Doch, ich bitte dich,
Eine Locke gib von deinem Haar.

Eben schlug die dumpfe Geisterstunde,
Und nun schien es ihr erst wohl zu sein.
Gierig schlürfte sie mit blassem Munde
Nun den dunkel blutgefärbten Wein;
Doch vom Weizenbrot,
Das er freundlich bot,
Nahm sie nicht den kleinsten Bissen ein.

Und dem Jüngling reichte sie die Schale,
Der, wie sie, nun hastig lüstern trank.
Liebe fordert er beim stillen Mahle;
Ach, sein armes Herz war liebekrank.
Doch sie widersteht,
Wie er immer fleht,
Bis er weinend auf das Bette sank.

"Me you shall not obtain, dear soul!
They intend you for my younger sister.
While I suffer torments in my silent cell,
ah, in her arms think of me,
the one who thinks only of you,
the one who feels hurt loving you;
she will soon be concealed in the earth!"

"No! I swear it by this flame,
which Hymen kindly shows us in advance:
you aren't lost to joy or lost to me,
you're coming with me to my father's house.
Darling, stay right here!
At once I'll celebrate with you
our unexpected wedding feast."

And already they exchange tokens of fidelity;
she hands him her golden chain
and he wants to hand her a cup,
silver, artistically wrought, without an equal.
"That is not for me;
but I beg you,
give me a lock of your hair."

The witching hour was just hollowly sounding,
and now for the first time she seemed to feel well.
Greedily now with her pale lips
she sipped the dark, blood-colored wine;
but of the wheat bread
that he amiably offered
she ate not the smallest bit.

And she handed the cup to the young man,
who, like her, now drank in sensual haste.
He asks her for love at the silent meal;
ah, his poor heart was sick with love.
But she resists,
no matter how often he beseeches her,
until he sank back on the bed weeping.

Und sie kommt und wirft sich zu ihm nieder:
Ach, wie ungern seh ich dich gequält!
Aber, ach! berührst du meine Glieder,
Fühlst du schaudernd, was ich dir verhehlt.
Wie der Schnee so weiß,
Aber kalt wie Eis
Ist das Liebchen, das du dir erwählt.

Heftig faßt er sie mit starken Armen,
Von der Liebe Jugendkraft durchmannt:
Hoffe doch, bei mir noch zu erwarmen,
Wärst du selbst mir aus dem Grab gesandt!
Wechselhauch und Kuß!
Liebesüberfluß!
Brennst du nicht und fühlest mich entbrannt?

Liebe schließet fester sie zusammen,
Tränen mischen sich in ihre Lust;
Gierig saugt sie seines Mundes Flammen,
Eins ist nur im andern sich bewußt.
Seine Liebeswut
Wärmt ihr starres Blut,
Doch es schlägt kein Herz in ihrer Brust.

Unterdessen schleichet auf dem Gange
Häuslich spät die Mutter noch vorbei,
Horchet an der Tür und horchet lange,
Welch ein sonderbarer Ton es sei:
Klag- und Wonnelaut
Bräutigams und Braut,
Und des Liebestammelns Raserei.

Unbeweglich bleibt sie an der Türe,
Weil sie erst sich überzeugen muß,
Und sie hört die höchsten Liebesschwüre,
Lieb und Schmeichelworte, mit Verdruß –
Still! der Hahn erwacht! –
Aber morgen Nacht
Bist du wieder da? – und Kuß auf Kuß.

And she comes and jumps down beside him:
"Oh, how I hate to see you in torment!
But, alas, if you touch my limbs,
you will feel with a shudder what I have concealed from you.
White as snow
but cold as ice
is the sweetheart you have chosen for yourself."

Violently he seizes her in his strong arms,
invigorated by love's youthful power:
"Expect to warm up here with me,
even if you were sent to me from the grave!
Exchange of breath and kisses!
Overflowing love!
Aren't you burning and can't you feel that I'm on fire?"

Love locks them more closely together,
tears are mingled with their pleasure;
greedily she drinks in the flames of his mouth,
each derives self-awareness only from the other.
His amorous fury
warms her sluggish blood,
but no heart beats in her breast.

Meanwhile in the corridor the mother
still comes stealing by, kept up late by domestic duties;
she listens at the door and listens long,
wondering what those peculiar sounds can be:
cries of lament and rapture
as of a bridegroom and a bride,
and the frenzied stammering of lovers.

Motionless she remains at the door,
because she must first be convinced,
and she hears the loftiest vows of love,
love and flattering words, with vexation—
"Quiet! the rooster is awakening!"
"But tomorrow night,
will you be back?"—and kiss upon kiss.

Länger hält die Mutter nicht das Zürnen,
Öffnet das bekannte Schloß geschwind: –
Gibt es hier im Hause solche Dirnen,
Die dem Fremden gleich zu Willen sind? –
So zur Tür hinein.
Bei der Lampe Schein
Sieht sie – Gott! sie sieht ihr eigen Kind.

Und der Jüngling will im ersten Schrecken
Mit des Mädchens eignem Schleierflor,
Mit dem Teppich die Geliebte decken;
Doch sie windet gleich sich selbst hervor.
Wie mit Geists Gewalt
Hebet die Gestalt
Lang und langsam sich im Bett empor.

Mutter! Mutter! spricht sie hohle Worte,
So mißgönnt Ihr mir die schöne Nacht!
Ihr vertreibt mich von dem warmen Orte.
Bin ich zur Verzweiflung nur erwacht?
Ists Euch nicht genug,
Daß ins Leichentuch,
Daß Ihr früh mich in das Grab gebracht?

Aber aus der schwerbedeckten Enge
Treibet mich ein eigenes Gericht.
Eurer Priester summende Gesänge
Und ihr Segen haben kein Gewicht;
Salz und Wasser kühlt
Nicht, wo Jugend fühlt;
Ach! die Erde kühlt die Liebe nicht.

Dieser Jüngling war mir erst versprochen,
Als noch Venus' heitrer Tempel stand.
Mutter, habt Ihr doch das Wort gebrochen,
Weil ein fremd, ein falsch Gelübd Euch band!
Doch kein Gott erhört,
Wenn die Mutter schwört,
Zu versagen ihrer Tochter Hand.

The mother can no longer contain her anger,
she quickly opens the familiar lock:
"Are there such harlots in this house
that yield to strangers immediately?"
And so she enters.
In the glow of the lamp
she sees—God! She sees her own child.

And in his first fright the young man
wishes to cover his sweetheart with the girl's own veil,
with the blanket,
but she immediately writhes out from under them.
As if with a spirit's power
the form stands up
slowly, erect on the bed.

"Mother, Mother!" her hollow words ring;
"so you begrudge me this beautiful night!
You drive me away from this warm spot.
Have I awakened only to despair?
Isn't it enough for you
that you brought me prematurely
to my shroud, to my grave?

"But from that heavily covered confinement
a law of my own chases me.
The humming chants of your priests
and their blessings have no weight;
salt and water don't afford coolness
where youthful feelings prevail;
ah, the earth doesn't cool down love.

"This young man was first promised to me
while Venus' cheerful temple still stood.
Mother, you broke your word
because a foreign, false vow hound you!
But no God hears
when a mother vows
to deny her daughter's hand.

Aus dem Grabe werd ich ausgetrieben,
Noch zu suchen das vermißte Gut,
Noch den schon verlornen Mann zu lieben
Und zu saugen seines Herzens Blut.
Ists um den geschehn,
Muß nach andern gehn,
Und das junge Volk erliegt der Wut.

Schöner Jüngling! kannst nicht länger leben;
Du versiechest nun an diesem Ort.
Meine Kette hab ich dir gegeben;
Deine Locke nehm ich mit mir fort.
Sieh sie an genau!
Morgen bist du grau,
Und nur braun erscheinst du wieder dort.

Höre, Mutter, nun die letzte Bitte:
Einen Scheiterhaufen schichte du;
Öffne meine bange kleine Hütte,
Bring in Flammen Liebende zur Ruh!
Wenn der Funke sprüht,
Wenn die Asche glüht,
Eilen wir den alten Göttern zu.

## Der Gott und die Bajadere
### Indische Legende

Mahadöh, der Herr der Erde,
Kommt herab zum sechsten Mal,
Daß er unsersgleichen werde,
Mit zu fühlen Freud und Qual.
Er bequemt sich, hier zu wohnen,
Läßt sich alles selbst geschehn.
Soll er strafen oder schonen,
Muß er Menschen menschlich sehn.
Und hat er die Stadt sich als Wandrer betrachtet,
Die Großen belauert, auf Kleine geachtet,
Verläßt er sie abends, um weiter zu gehn.

"I am driven out of the grave,
to continue seeking the good things I missed,
to continue loving the man already lost,
and to suck his heart's blood.
If he is now doomed,
I must go after others,
and our young men will succumb to my fury.

"Handsome youth! You can no longer live;
you will now waste away on this spot.
I've given you my chain;
I shall take your lock of hair away with me.
Take a close look at it!
Tomorrow you'll be gray,
and only *there* will your hair be brown again.

"Now, Mother, hear my last request:
build a pyre;
open my fearful little cabin,
give lovers repose in the flames!
When the sparks fly,
when the ashes smoulder,
we shall hasten away to the old gods."

# The God and the Bayadere
## Legend of India

Mahadeva, lord of the earth,
descends for the sixth time,
to become like one of us,
to feel joy and torment like us.
He deigns to dwell here,
leaving all events to take their own course.
If he is to punish or be lenient,
he must see human beings with their own eyes.
And after studying the city in the guise of a wayfarer,
spying on its great men and observing the small,
he leaves it in the evening to continue his journey.

Als er nun hinausgegangen,
Wo die letzten Häuser sind,
Sieht er, mit gemalten Wangen,
Ein verlornes schönes Kind.
Grüß dich, Jungfrau! – Dank der Ehre!
Wart, ich komme gleich hinaus –
Und wer bist du? – Bajadere,
Und dies ist der Liebe Haus.
Sie rührt sich, die Zimbeln zum Tanze zu schlagen,
Sie weiß sich so lieblich im Kreise zu tragen,
Sie neigt sich und biegt sich und reicht ihm den Strauß.

Schmeichelnd zieht sie ihn zur Schwelle,
Lebhaft ihn ins Haus hinein.
Schöner Fremdling, lampenhelle
Soll sogleich die Hütte sein.
Bist du müd, ich will dich laben,
Lindern deiner Füße Schmerz.
Was du willst, das sollst du haben,
Ruhe, Freuden oder Scherz.
Sie lindert geschäftig geheuchelte Leiden.
Der Göttliche lächelt; er siehet mit Freuden
Durch tiefes Verderben ein menschliches Herz.

Und er fordert Sklavendienste;
Immer heitrer wird sie nur,
Und des Mädchens frühe Künste
Werden nach und nach Natur.
Und so stellet auf die Blüte
Bald und bald die Frucht sich ein;
Ist Gehorsam im Gemüte,
Wird nicht fern die Liebe sein.
Aber, sie schärfer und schärfer zu prüfen,
Wählet der Kenner der Höhen und Tiefen
Lust und Entsetzen und grimmige Pein.

Und er küßt die bunten Wangen
Und sie fühlt der Liebe Qual,
Und das Mädchen steht gefangen,
Und sie weint zum erstenmal;
Sinkt zu seinen Füßen nieder,

Now that he has gone out
where the last houses stand,
he sees a beautiful fallen girl
with painted cheeks.
"Greetings, maiden!" "Thanks for the honor!
Wait, I'm coming right out."
"And who are you?" "A bayadere,
and this is the house of love."
She bestirs herself to beat the cymbals for the dance;
she knows how to whirl around so charmingly,
she bows and stoops and hands him her bouquet.

Flatteringly she draws him toward the threshold,
briskly she draws him into the house.
"Handsome stranger, my cottage
will be bright with lamps at once.
If you are weary, I shall refresh you
and soothe the pain of your feet.
Whatever you wish you shall have,
Rest, pleasures, or sport."
She busily soothes feigned suffering.
The divine one smiles; he sees with joy
a humane heart beneath her deep corruption.

And he demands services as if from a slave;
but she merely becomes more cheerful,
and what were previously the girl's artful practices
gradually become natural to her.
And so the blossom
is soon followed by the fruit;
if obedience is in one's mind,
love will not be far off.
But, in order to test her more and more fully,
the knower of the heights and depths chooses
pleasure and horror and bitter pain.

And he kisses her painted cheeks,
and she feels the torment of love,
and the girl is a prisoner there,
and she weeps for the first time;
she sinks down at his feet,

Nicht um Wollust noch Gewinst,
Ach! und die gelenken Glieder,
Sie versagen allen Dienst.
Und so zu des Lagers vergnüglicher Feier
Bereiten den dunklen behaglichen Schleier
Die nächtlichen Stunden, das schöne Gespinst.

Spät entschlummert unter Scherzen,
Früh erwacht nach kurzer Rast,
Findet sie an ihrem Herzen
Tot den vielgeliebten Gast.
Schreiend stürzt sie auf ihn nieder,
Aber nicht erweckt sie ihn;
Und man trägt die starren Glieder
Bald zur Flammengrube hin.
Sie höret die Priester, die Totengesänge,
Sie raset und rennet und teilet die Menge.
Wer bist du? was drängt zu der Grube dich hin?

Bei der Bahre stürzt sie nieder,
Ihr Geschrei durchdringt die Luft:
Meinen Gatten will ich wieder!
Und ich such ihn in der Gruft.
Soll zu Asche mir zerfallen
Dieser Glieder Götterpracht?
Mein! er war es, mein vor allen!
Ach, nur Eine süße Nacht!
Es singen die Priester: Wir tragen die Alten,
Nach langem Ermatten und spätem Erkalten,
Wir tragen die Jugend, noch eh sies gedacht.

Höre deiner Priester Lehre:
Dieser war dein Gatte nicht.
Lebst du doch als Bajadere,
Und so hast du keinen Pflicht.
Nur dem Körper folgt der Schatten
In das stille Totenreich;
Nur die Gattin folgt dem Gatten:
Das ist Pflicht und Ruhm zugleich.
Ertöne, Drommete, zu heiliger Klage!
O nehmet, ihr Götter! die Zierde der Tage,
O nehmet den Jüngling in Flammen zu euch!

not for lust or profit,
alas, and her supple limbs
deny her any service.
And so for the enjoyable ceremony of the couch
the night hours prepare their dark,
comforting veil, that beautiful fabric.

After falling asleep late amidst their play,
awakening early after a brief rest,
she finds the dearly beloved guest
lying dead on her bosom.
Shrieking, she throws herself upon him,
but she cannot waken him;
and his stiff limbs
are soon carried out to the fiery pit.
She hears the priests, the funeral chants,
she raves and runs and parts the throng.
"Who are you? What impels you to the pyre?"

She collapses near the bier,
her cries pierce the air:
"I want my husband back,
and I seek him in the grave!
Shall the godlike splendor of those limbs
crumble to ashes?
Mine! He was mine above all others!
Ah, only one sweet night!"
The priests chant: "We carry the old,
after they have long grown weary and belatedly grown cold;
we carry the young sooner than they expected.

"Hear the teachings of your priests:
This man was not your husband.
After all, you live as a bayadere
and so you have no responsibilities toward him.
Only the shade follows the body
into the silent realm of the dead;
only the wife follows the husband:
that is a duty and an honor at the same time.
Sound, trumpet, a sacred lament!
Take, you gods, the ornament of our days,
take this youth unto yourselves in flames!"

So das Chor, das ohn Erbarmen
Mehret ihres Herzens Not;
Und mit ausgestreckten Armen
Springt sie in den heißen Tod.
Doch der Götter-Jüngling hebet
Aus der Flamme sich empor,
Und in seinen Armen schwebet
Die Geliebte mit hervor.
Es freut sich die Gottheit der reuigen Sünder;
Unsterbliche heben verlorene Kinder
Mit feurigen Armen zum Himmel empor.

## Der Zauberlehrling

Hat der alte Hexenmeister
Sich doch einmal weggebegeben!
Und nun sollen seine Geister
Auch nach meinem Willen leben.
Seine Wort' und Werke
Merkt ich und den Brauch,
Und mit Geistesstärke
Tu ich Wunder auch.

    Walle! walle
    Manche Strecke,
    Daß, zum Zwecke,
    Wasser fließe
    Und mit reichem, vollem Schwalle
    Zu dem Bade sich ergieße.

Und nun komm, du alter Besen!
Nimm die schlechten Lumpenhüllen;
Bist schon lange Knecht gewesen:
Nun erfülle meinen Willen!
Auf zwei Beinen stehe,
Oben sei ein Kopf,
Eile nun und gehe
Mit dem Wassertopf!

Thus sings the chorus, which pitilessly
increases her heart's distress;
and with outstretched arms
she leaps into the hot death.
But the divine youth rises
out of the flames,
and in his arms his loved one
soars upward with him.
The godhead rejoices over repentant sinners;
immortals raise fallen children
up to heaven in fiery arms.

## The Sorcerer's Apprentice

The old sorcerer
has finally gone out!
And now his spirits
shall live in accordance with *my* wishes, too.
I paid attention to his spells
and actions, and how to use them,
and with the strength of spirits
I shall work wonders, too.

Surge! surge
many a stretch,
so that, for my purposes,
water may flow
and, with an abundant, full gush,
pour itself out for a bath.

And now come, you old broom!
Take these rough, ragged coverings;
you've already been a servant for a long time:
now fulfill my wishes!
Stand on two legs,
let there be a head on top;
now hurry and walk
with the pot of water!

Walle! walle
Manche Strecke,
Daß, zum Zwecke,
Wasser fließe
Und mit reichem, vollem Schwalle
Zu dem Bade sich ergieße.

Seht, er läuft zum Ufer nieder,
Wahrlich! ist schon an dem Flusse,
Und mit Blitzesschnelle wieder
Ist er hier mit raschem Gusse.
Schon zum zweiten Male!
Wie das Becken schwillt!
Wie sich jede Schale
Voll mit Wasser füllt!

Stehe! stehe!
Denn wir haben
Deiner Gaben
Vollgemessen! –
Ach, ich merk es! Wehe! wehe!
Hab ich doch das Wort vergessen!

Ach, das Wort, worauf am Ende
Er das wird, was er gewesen.
Ach, er läuft und bringt behende!
Wärst du doch der alte Besen!
Immer neue Güsse
Bringt er schnell herein,
Ach! und hundert Flüsse
Stürzen auf mich ein.

Nein, nicht länger
Kann ichs lassen;
Will ihn fassen.
Das ist Tücke!
Ach! nun wird mir immer bänger!
Welche Miene! welche Blicke!

Surge! surge
many a stretch,
so that, for my purposes,
water may flow
and, with an abundant, full gush,
pour itself out for a bath.

See, it runs down to the river bank;
truly! it's already at the river,
and, with the speed of lightning, it's back
here with a rapid outpouring.
For the second time now!
How the water rises in the tub!
How every basin
is filled with water!

Stop! Stop!
For we have
the full measure
of your gifts!—
Ah, I can see! Woe! Woe!
I've forgotten the magic spell!—

ah, the spell by which it finally
becomes again what it was before.
Ah, it runs and swiftly brings more!
If you were only the old broom!
It quickly brings in
more and more loads of water,
ah, and a hundred rivers
are crashing onto me.

No, no longer
can I let this go on;
I must grab it.
This is spitework!
Ah, now I'm getting more and more scared!
What an expression! What looks!

O, du Ausgeburt der Hölle!
Soll das ganze Haus ersaufen?
Seh ich über jede Schwelle
Doch schon Wasserströme laufen.
Ein verruchter Besen,
Der nicht hören will!
Stock, der du gewesen,
Steh doch wieder still!

Willsts am Ende
Gar nicht lassen?
Will dich fassen,
Will dich halten
Und das alte Holz behende
Mit dem scharfen Beile spalten.

Seht, da kommt er schleppend wieder!
Wie ich mich nur auf dich werfe,
Gleich, o Kobold, liegst du nieder;
Krachend trifft die glatte Schärfe.
Wahrlich! brav getroffen!
Seht, er ist entzwei!
Und nun kann ich hoffen,
Und ich atme frei!

Wehe! wehe!
Beide Teile
Stehn in Eile
Schon als Knechte
Völlig fertig in die Höhe!
Helft mir, ach! ihr hohen Mächte!

Und sie laufen! Naß und nässer
Wirds im Saal und auf den Stufen.
Welch entsetzliches Gewässer!
Herr und Meister! hör mich rufen! –
Ach, da kommt der Meister!
Herr, die Not ist groß!
Die ich rief, die Geister
Werd ich nun nicht los.

Oh, you offspring of hell!
Will the whole house be drowned?
After all, I already see streams of water
running over every threshold.
A wicked broom
that won't obey!
Stick that you were,
won't you stand still again?

Won't you finally
give it up?
I'll grab you,
I'll hold you
and quickly split the old wood
with this sharp hatchet.

Look, here he comes hauling water again!
As soon as I jump on you,
you goblin, you'll be vanquished at once;
with a crash the smooth edge hits you.
Truly! A direct hit!
Look, it's cut in two!
And now I can hope again,
and I breathe freely!

Woe! Woe!
Both parts
quickly stand up
erect again,
all complete, as servants!
Ah, help me, you divine powers!

And they run! Wet and wetter
it becomes in the chamber and on the stairs.
What a horrible flood!
Lord and master! Hear me calling you!—
Ah, here comes my master!
Sir, the peril is great!
The spirits I summoned
I now can't get rid of.

»In die Ecke,
Besen! Besen!
Seids gewesen.
Denn als Geister
Ruft euch nur, zu diesem Zwecke,
Erst hervor der alte Meister.«

## Der Musensohn

Durch Feld und Wald zu schweifen,
Mein Liedchen wegzupfeifen,
So gehts von Ort zu Ort!
Und nach dem Takte reget,
Und nach dem Maß beweget
Sich alles an mir fort.

Ich kann sie kaum erwarten,
Die erste Blum im Garten,
Die erste Blüt am Baum.
Sie grüßen meine Lieder,
Und kommt der Winter wieder,
Sing ich noch jenen Traum.

Ich sing ihn in der Weite,
Auf Eises Läng und Breite,
Da blüht der Winter schön!
Auch diese Blüte schwindet,
Und neue Freude findet
Sich auf bebauten Höhn.

Denn wie ich bei der Linde
Das junge Völkchen finde,
Sogleich erreg ich sie.
Der stumpfe Bursche bläht sich,
Das steife Mädchen dreht sich
Nach meiner Melodie.

Ihr gebt den Sohlen Flügel
Und treibt durch Tal und Hügel
Den Liebling weit von Haus.

"Into the corner,
brooms, brooms!
You are no longer what you were.
For as spirits,
for such a purpose, only the old master
will summon you again."

## The Son of the Muses

To roam through fields and forest,
to pipe my little song,
that's how it goes from one place to another!
And everything stirs to my beat,
and everything moves along with me
to my measure.

I can hardly wait to see them,
the first flower in the garden,
the first blossom on the tree.
They welcome my songs,
and when winter comes again,
I still sing about that dream.

I sing of it all around,
on the length and breadth of the ice,
and then winter puts forth beautiful blossoms!
That blossoming vanishes, too,
and new joy is found
on plowed uplands.

For, when I find
young folks by the linden tree,
I enliven them at once.
The stolid fellow is puffed up with importance,
the stiffly formal girl whirls around
to my melody.

You lend wings to my soles
and drive your favorite far from home
over valleys and hills.

Ihr lieben holden Musen,
Wann ruh ich ihr am Busen
Auch endlich wieder aus?

## [Sonett]

Natur und Kunst, sie scheinen sich zu fliehen
   Und haben sich, eh man es denkt, gefunden;
   Der Widerwille ist auch mir verschwunden,
   Und beide scheinen gleich mich anzuziehen.

Es gilt wohl nur ein redliches Bemühen!
   Und wenn wir erst in abgemeßnen Stunden
   Mit Geist und Fleiß uns an die Kunst gebunden,
   Mag frei Natur im Herzen wieder glühen.

So ists mit aller Bildung auch beschaffen:
   Vergebens werden ungebundne Geister
   Nach der Vollendung reiner Höhe streben.

Wer Großes will, muß sich zusammenraffen;
   In der Beschränkung zeigt sich erst der Meister,
   Und das Gesetz nur kann uns Freiheit geben.

## Tischlied

Mich ergreift, ich weiß nicht wie,
Himmlisches Behagen.
Will michs etwa gar hinauf
Zu den Sternen tragen?
Doch ich bleibe lieber hier,
Kann ich redlich sagen,
Beim Gesang und Glase Wein
Auf den Tisch zu schlagen.

Wundert euch, ihr Freunde, nicht,
Wie ich mich gebärde;
Wirklich ist es allerliebst
Auf der lieben Erde:

You dear, sweet Muses,
when will I finally find rest again
on her breast?

## [Sonnet]

Nature and art seem to shun each other
    but are joined up before you expect it;
    I've lost the sense of opposition, too,
    and both seem to attract me equally.

Surely, all it takes is an honest effort!
    And, if we first, at allotted hours,
    have bound ourselves to art with intelligence and diligence,
    nature can freely glow in our heart again.

That's how it is with all creative development:
    in vain will undisciplined minds
    strive for the pure heights of perfection.

Whoever wishes to accomplish great things must pull himself together;
    it is only within constraints that mastery can show itself,
    and only law can give us liberty.

## Banquet Song

I am seized, I know not how,
by heavenly contentment.
Will I perhaps even be
carried up to the stars?
But I'd rather stay here,
I can honestly say,
banging on the table
amid singing and with a glass of wine.

Don't be surprised, friends,
at my behavior;
truly it's the dearest thing of all
to be on the dear earth:

Darum schwör ich feierlich
Und ohn alle Fährde,
Daß ich mich nicht freventlich
Wegbegeben werde.

Da wir aber allzumal
So beisammen weilen,
Dächt ich, klänge der Pokal
Zu des Dichters Zeilen.
Gute Freunde ziehen fort,
Wohl ein hundert Meilen,
Darum soll man hier am Ort
Anzustoßen eilen.

Lebe hoch, wer Leben schafft!
Das ist meine Lehre.
Unser König denn voran,
Ihm gebührt die Ehre.
Gegen inn- und äußern Feind
Setzt er sich zur Wehre;
Ans Erhalten denkt er zwar,
Mehr noch, wie er mehre.

Nun begrüß ich sie sogleich,
Sie, die einzig Eine.
Jeder denke ritterlich
Sich dabei die Seine.
Merket auch ein schönes Kind,
Wen ich eben meine,
Nun, so nicke sie mir zu:
Leb auch so der Meine!

Freunden gilt das dritte Glas,
Zweien oder dreien,
Die mit uns am guten Tag
Sich im stillen freuen
Und der Nebel trübe Nacht
Leis und leicht zerstreuen;
Diesen sei ein Hoch gebracht,
Alten oder neuen.

therefore I swear solemnly,
and without any guile,
that I shall not steal away
criminally.

But since we are tarrying
all together here,
I think the goblets should clink
to the poet's lines.
Good friends go away,
for some hundred miles,
and so, here where we are,
we should hasten to clink glasses.

Long live the man who gives us life!
That's my doctrine.
And so, our king first of all,
he deserves that honor.
Against internal and external enemies
he offers resistance;
to be sure, he thinks about preserving what he has,
but even more about how he can increase it.

Now I at once greet her,
her, the one and only.
Let every man think chivalrously
of his own lady as I say this.
If some beautiful girl realizes
whom I happen to mean,
well, let her nod to me:
"Long live my lover, too!"

The third glass is to friends,
just two or three,
who rejoice with us
silently on good days
and softly and lightly dispel
the night that is gloomy with mists;
let a "long live" be said for them,
whether they are old friends or new.

Breiter wallet nun der Strom,
Mit vermehrten Wellen.
Leben jetzt im hohen Ton
Redliche Gesellen!
Die sich mit gedrängter Kraft
Brav zusammen stellen
In des Glückes Sonnenschein
Und in schlimmen Fällen.

Wie wir nun zusammen sind,
Sind zusammen viele.
Wohl gelingen denn, wie uns,
Andern ihre Spiele!
Von der Quelle bis ans Meer
Mahlet manche Mühle,
Und das Wohl der ganzen Welt
Ists, worauf ich ziele.

## Schäfers Klagelied

Da droben auf jenem Berge,
Da steh ich tausendmal,
An meinem Stabe gebogen,
Und schaue hinab in das Tal.

Dann folg ich der weidenden Herde,
Mein Hündchen bewahret mir sie.
Ich bin herunter gekommen
Und weiß doch selber nicht wie.

Da stehet von schönen Blumen
Die ganze Wiese so voll.
Ich breche sie, ohne zu wissen,
Wem ich sie geben soll.

Und Regen, Sturm und Gewitter
Verpaß ich unter dem Baum.
Die Türe dort bleibet verschlossen;
Denn alles ist leider ein Traum.

Now the current surges more broadly,
with increased waves.
Now, in loud tones, long live
honest companions,
who with compact strength
uprightly join forces with us
in the sunshine of good fortune
and on unhappy occasions.

Just as we are together now,
many groups are together.
And so, may others succeed
in their activities just as we do!
From the source to the sea
many a mill grinds,
and the well-being of the whole world
is what I aim for.

## Shepherd's Song of Lament

Up there on yonder mountain,
I stand a thousand times
leaning on my staff
and looking down at the valley.

Then I follow my grazing flock,
my little dog guards it for me.
I've come all the way down,
and I myself don't know how it happened.

Here the whole meadow is so full
of beautiful flowers.
I pick them without knowing
to whom I should give them.

And I wait under the tree
for rain, storm, and thunder to go by.
The door there remains locked;
for unfortunately it's all a dream.

Es stehet ein Regenbogen
Wohl über jenem Haus!
Sie aber ist weggezogen,
Und weit in das Land hinaus.

Hinaus in das Land und weiter,
Vielleicht gar über die See.
Vorüber, ihr Schafe, vorüber!
Dem Schäfer ist gar so weh.

## Epilog zu Schillers Glocke

Freude dieser Stadt bedeute,
Friede sei ihr erst Geläute!

Und so geschahs! Dem friedenreichen Klange
Bewegte sich das Land, und segenbar
Ein frisches Glück erschien: im Hochgesange
Begrüßten wir das junge Fürstenpaar;
Im Vollgewühl, in lebensregem Drange
Vermischte sich die tätge Völkerschar,
Und festlich ward an die geschmückten Stufen
Die *Huldigung der Künste* vorgerufen.

Da hör ich schreckhaft mitternächtges Läuten,
Das dumpf und schwer die Trauertöne schwellt.
Ists möglich? Soll es unsern Freund bedeuten,
An den sich jeder Wunsch geklammert hält?
Den Lebenswürdgen soll der Tod erbeuten?
Ach! wie verwirrt solch ein Verlust die Welt!
Ach! was zerstört ein solcher Riß den Seinen!
Nun weint die Welt, und sollten wir nicht weinen?

Denn er war unser! Wie bequem gesellig
Den hohen Mann der gute Tag gezeigt,
Wie bald sein Ernst, anschließend, wohlgefällig,
Zur Wechselrede heiter sich geneigt,
Bald raschgewandt, geistreich und sicherstellig
Der Lebensplane tiefen Sinn erzeugt
Und fruchtbar sich in Rat und Tat ergossen:
Das haben wir erfahren und genossen.

A rainbow is arching
over that house!
But she has gone away,
to a far distant place.

To a distant place, and even farther,
perhaps even over the sea.
Pass by, sheep, pass by!
The shepherd is so very sad.

## *Epilogue to Schiller's "Song of the Bell"*

May it mean joy for this city,
may its first ringing be for peace!

And so it came to pass! To that peace-bearing sound
the land bestirred itself, and, rich in blessings,
a new happiness appeared: in a sacred hymn
we greeted the young princely couple;
in busy turmoil, in a lively burst of activity
the industrious group of nations intermingled,
and festively the *Homage of the Arts*
was summoned to the decorated stage.

Then I hear frightful tolling at midnight,
with tones of mourning swelling hollowly and heavily.
Is it possible? Is it intended for our friend,
to whom everyone's good wishes cling?
Shall death make that man, so deserving of life, its prey?
Ah, how a loss like that confuses the world!
Ah, what a laceration like that destroys for his friends!
Now the world weeps, and are we not to weep?

For he belonged to us! How obligingly sociable
that noble man proved to be in fortunate times;
how, at one moment, his earnestness, accommodating and eager to please,
cheerfully made itself open to a dialogue;
and at another moment, quickly resourceful, intelligent, and sure in its judgments,
it engendered the profound wisdom of plans for life
and fruitfully poured itself forth in advice and deeds:
that, we experienced and enjoyed.

Denn er war unser! Mag das stolze Wort
Den lauten Schmerz gewaltig übertönen!
Er mochte sich bei uns, im sichern Port,
Nach wildem Sturm zum Dauernden gewöhnen.
Indessen schritt sein Geist gewaltig fort
Ins Ewige des Wahren, Guten, Schönen,
Und hinter ihm, in wesenlosem Scheine,
Lag, was uns alle bändigt, das Gemeine.

Nun schmückt' er sich die schöne Gartenzinne,
Von wannen er der Sterne Wort vernahm,
Das dem gleich ewgen, gleich lebendgen Sinne
Geheimnisvoll und klar entgegenkam.
Dort, sich und uns zu köstlichem Gewinne,
Verwechselt' er die Zeiten wundersam,
Begegnet' so, im Würdigsten beschäftigt,
Der Dämmerung, der Nacht, die uns entkräftigt.

Ihm schwollen der Geschichte Flut- auf Fluten,
Verspülend, was getadelt, was gelobt,
Der Erdbeherrscher wilde Heeresgluten,
Die in der Welt sich grimmig ausgetobt,
Im niedrig Schrecklichsten, im höchsten Guten
Nach ihrem Wesen deutlich durchgeprobt. –
Nun sank der Mond, und zu erneuter Wonne
Vom klaren Berg herüber stieg die Sonne.

Nun glühte seine Wange rot und röter
Von jener Jugend, die uns nie entfliegt,
Von jenem Mut, der, früher oder später,
Den Widerstand der stumpfen Welt besiegt,
Von jenem Glauben, der sich, stets erhöhter,
Bald kühn hervordrängt, bald geduldig schmiegt,
Damit das Gute wirke, wachse, fromme,
Damit der Tag dem Edlen endlich komme.

Doch hat er, so geübt, so vollgehaltig,
Dies bretterne Gerüste nicht verschmäht;
Hier schildert er das Schicksal, das gewaltig
Von Tag zu Nacht die Erdenachse dreht,

For he belonged to us! May that proud word
powerfully drown out our loud sorrow!
He was pleased, after wild storms, to accustom himself
to a settled condition here with us, in a safe haven.
Meanwhile his mind powerfully continued on
into the eternal realm of the true, good, and beautiful;
and, abandoned behind him, as an unsubstantial sham,
lay that which subdues us all: the vulgar and commonplace.

Now he adorned for himself that lovely garden house with its tower,
from which he heard the words of the stars,
which mysteriously but clearly corresponded
to his equally eternal, equally lively mind.
There, to his precious profit and to ours,
he marvelously interchanged times and seasons,
and thus, occupied in the worthiest tasks, he met
the twilight, the night that robs us of our strength.

For him the tides of history rose up one after another,
carrying along with them the blameworthy, the praiseworthy,
the wild military fires of the rulers of the earth,
which burnt themselves out so fiercely in the world,
all clearly investigated in accordance with their essence,
to the depths of horror, to the heights of goodness.—
Now the moon set, and to renewed rapture
the sun rose toward us from the bright mountain.

Now his cheeks burned redder and redder
with that youth which never deserts us,
with that courage which sooner or later
conquers the resistance of the stolid world,
with that faith which, ever increasing,
now pushes forward boldly, now patiently adapts itself,
so that the good can take effect, grow, and be useful,
so that the day of the noble man can finally arrive.

But, with that training, with all those talents,
he didn't scorn this wooden platform;
here he portrayed the fate that mightily
turns the earth's axis from day to night,

Und manches tiefe Werk hat, reichgestaltig,
Den Wert der Kunst, des Künstlers Wert erhöht.
Er wendete die Blüte höchsten Strebens,
Das Leben selbst, an dieses Bild des Lebens.

Ihr kanntet ihn, wie er mit Riesenschritte
Den Kreis des Wollens, des Vollbringens maß,
Durch Zeit und Land, der Völker Sinn und Sitte,
Das dunkle Buch mit heiterm Blicke las;
Doch wie er atemlos in unsrer Mitte
In Leiden bangte, kümmerlich genas,
Das haben wir in traurig schönen Jahren,
Denn er war unser, leidend miterfahren.

Ihn, wenn er vom zerrüttenden Gewühle
Des bittern Schmerzes wieder aufgeblickt,
Ihn haben wir dem lästigen Gefühle
Der Gegenwart, der stockenden, entrückt,
Mit guter Kunst und ausgesuchtem Spiele
Den neubelebten edlen Sinn erquickt
Und noch am Abend vor den letzten Sonnen
Ein holdes Lächeln glücklich abgewonnen.

Er hatte früh das strenge Wort gelesen,
Dem Leiden war er, war dem Tod vertraut.
So schied er nun, wie er so oft genesen;
Nun schreckt uns das, wofür uns längst gegraut.
Doch schon erblicket sein verklärtes Wesen
Sich hier verklärt, wenn es hernniederschaut.
Was Mitwelt sonst an ihm beklagt, getadelt,
Es hats der Tod, es hats die Zeit geadelt.

Auch manche Geister, die mit ihm gerungen,
Sein groß Verdienst unwillig anerkannt,
Sie fühlen sich von seiner Kraft durchdrungen,
In seinem Kreise willig festgebannt:
Zum Höchsten hat er sich emporgeschwungen,
Mit allem, was wir schätzen, eng verwandt.
So feiert Ihn! Denn was dem Mann das Leben
Nur halb erteilt, soll ganz die Nachwelt geben.

and many a profound work, rich in characters,
enhanced the value of art, the artist's value.
He applied the flower of his loftiest ambition,
life itself, to this image of life.

You knew him, you saw how with giant steps
he took the measure of the cycle of wishing and accomplishing,
how with serene eyes he read the obscure book
of times and places, the thoughts and customs of the nations;
but also how in our midst, breathlessly,                       .
he suffered anxiety in his illness, making only incomplete recoveries:
that, in those sadly beautiful years, we
were sorrowful witnesses to, for he belonged to us.

Whenever he looked up again
after the exhausting turmoil of bitter pain,
we rescued him from the burdensome emotions
of the stagnating present moment;
with worthy art and exquisite acting
we revived and refreshed that noble mind;
and even on the evening before his last sunrise
we were lucky enough to elicit a charming smile from him.

Early on, he had read that severe word;
he was familiar with suffering, with death.
And so he departed just as he had so often recovered;
now we are dismayed by that which we so long feared.
But his transfigured being already sees
itself transfigured here, if it looks down.
What his fellow men may have lamented or found fault with in him
has been ennobled by death and time.

Even the many spirits who fought against him,
unwillingly acknowledging his great merit,
feel themselves permeated with his strength,
willingly spellbound in his magic circle:
he raised himself up to the greatest heights,
closely associated with all that we prize.
And so, honor him! For that which is only half bestowed
on a man while he lives, should be given totally by posterity.

So bleibt er uns, der vor so manchen Jahren –
Schon zehne sinds! – von uns sich weggekehrt!
Wir alle haben segenreich erfahren,
Die Welt verdank ihm, was er sie gelehrt;
Schon längst verbreitet sichs in ganze Scharen,
Das Eigenste, was ihm allein gehört.
Er glänzt uns vor, wie ein Komet entschwindend,
Unendlich Licht mit seinem Licht verbindend.

## *Vanitas! vanitatum vanitas!*

Ich hab mein Sach auf Nichts gestellt.
     Juchhe!
Drum ist so wohl mir in der Welt.
     Juchhe!
Und wer will mein Kamerade sein,
Der stoße mit an, der stimme mit ein
Bei dieser Neige Wein.

Ich stellt mein Sach auf Geld und Gut.
     Juchhe!
Darüber verlor ich Freud und Mut.
     O weh!
Die Münze rollte hier und dort,
Und hascht ich sie an einem Ort,
Am andern war sie fort.

Auf Weiber stellt ich nun mein Sach.
     Juchhe!
Daher mir kam viel Ungemach.
     O weh!
Die Falsche sucht' sich ein ander Teil,
Die Treue macht' mir Langeweil,
Die Beste war nicht feil.

Ich stellt mein Sach auf Reis' und Fahrt.
     Juchhe!
Und ließ meine Vaterlandesart.
     O weh!

And so he remains with us, he that turned away from us
so many years ago—it's already ten!
We have all learned it with blessings,
let the world thank him for what he taught it.
For a long time now, the unique gifts that were his alone
have spread abroad to wide circles of people.
He shines before us, vanishing like a comet,
joining the infinite light to his own light.

## Vanity! Vanity of Vanities!

I've hitched my wagon to nothing.
                    Hurray!
That's why I feel so good in the world.
                    Hurray!
And whoever wants to be my comrade,
let him clink glasses with me, let him sing with me
while drinking the last wine in the glass.

I hitched my wagon to money and property.
                    Hurray!
And I lost my joy and my courage over it.
                    Oh, woe!
The coin rolled here and there,
and if I grabbed it in one place,
it was gone in another.

Then I hitched my wagon to women.
                    Hurray!
That caused me a lot of trouble.
                    Oh, woe!
The false woman looked for another partner,
the faithful one bored me,
the best one of all wasn't for sale.

I hitched my wagon to journeys and travel.
                    Hurray!
And left behind the customs of my native country.
                    Oh, woe!

Und mir behagt' es nirgends recht,
Die Kost war fremd, das Bett war schlecht,
Niemand verstand mich recht.

Ich stellt mein Sach auf Ruhm und Ehr.
                    Juchhe!
Und sieh! gleich hatt ein andrer mehr.
                    O weh!
Wie ich mich hatt hervorgetan,
Da sahen die Leute scheel mich an,
Hatte keinem recht getan.

Ich setzt mein Sach auf Kampf und Krieg.
                    Juchhe!
Und uns gelang so mancher Sieg.
                    Juchhe!
Wir zogen in Feindes Land hinein,
Dem Freunde sollts nicht viel besser sein,
Und ich verlor ein Bein.

Nun hab ich mein Sach auf Nichts gestellt.
                    Juchhe!
Und mein gehört die ganze Welt.
                    Juchhe!
Zu Ende geht nun Sang und Schmaus.
Nur trinkt mir alle Neigen aus;
Die letzte muß heraus!

## Metamorphose der Tiere

Wagt ihr, also bereitet, die letzte Stufe zu steigen
Dieses Gipfels, so reicht mir die Hand und öffnet den freien
Blick ins weite Feld der Natur. Sie spendet die reichen
Lebensgaben umher, die Göttin; aber empfindet
Keine Sorge wie sterbliche Fraun um ihrer Gebornen
Sichere Nahrung; ihr ziemet es nicht; denn zwiefach bestimmte
Sie das höchste Gesetz, beschränkte jegliches Leben,
Gab ihm gemeßnes Bedürfnis, und ungemessene Gaben,
Leicht zu finden, streute sie aus, und ruhig begünstigt
Sie das muntre Bemühn der vielfach bedürftigen Kinder;
Unerzogen schwärmen sie fort nach ihrer Bestimmung.

And I was never really comfortable anywhere;
the food was unfamiliar, the bed was no good,
no one really understood me.

I hitched my wagon to fame and honor.
                    Hurray!
And look! Right away, others had more.
                    Oh, woe!
As soon as I distinguished myself,
people looked at me enviously;
nothing I did was right for anybody.

I hitched my wagon to battle and war.
                    Hurray!
And we were victorious so often.
                    Hurray!
We marched into the enemy's country,
but things weren't much better for us friends,
and I lost a leg.

Now I've hitched my wagon to nothing.
                    Hurray!
And the whole world belongs to me.
                    Hurray!
Song and feast are now coming to an end.
Now all of you, finish the wine in your glasses;
the last drop must go!

# Metamorphosis of Animals

If, thus prepared, you will venture to climb the final stage
of this summit, give me your hand and look freely
at the wide field of nature. She bestows the rich
gifts of life all around, that goddess; but she feels
no worry, as mortal women do, about assuring nourishment
for her offspring; that doesn't befit her; for in two ways she decreed
the highest law, setting limits to each form of life,
giving it restricted needs and strewing about
unrestricted resources, easily found; and calmly she favors
the lively efforts of her children, who have various needs;
without upbringing they roam about in accordance with their predestination.

Zweck sein selbst ist jegliches Tier, vollkommen entspringt es
Aus dem Schoß der Natur und zeugt vollkommene Kinder.
Alle Glieder bilden sich aus nach ewgen Gesetzen,
Und die seltenste Form bewahrt im geheimen das Urbild.
So ist jeglicher Mund geschickt, die Speise zu fassen,
Welche dem Körper gebührt; es sei nun schwächlich und zahnlos
Oder mächtig der Kiefer gezähnt, in jeglichem Falle
Fördert ein schicklich Organ den übrigen Gliedern die Nahrung.
Auch bewegt sich jeglicher Fuß, der lange, der kurze,
Ganz harmonisch zum Sinne des Tiers und seinem Bedürfnis.
So ist jedem der Kinder die volle, reine Gesundheit
Von der Mutter bestimmt: denn alle lebendigen Glieder
Widersprechen sich nie und wirken alle zum Leben.
Also bestimmt die Gestalt die Lebensweise des Tieres,
Und die Weise zu leben, sie wirkt auf alle Gestalten
Mächtig zurück. So zeigt sich fest die geordnete Bildung,
Welche zum Wechsel sich neigt durch äußerlich wirkende Wesen.
Doch im Innern befindet die Kraft der edlern Geschöpfe
Sich im heiligen Kreise lebendiger Bildung beschlossen.
Diese Grenzen erweitert kein Gott, es ehrt die Natur sie:
Denn nur also beschränkt war je das Vollkommene möglich.

Doch im Innern scheint ein Geist gewaltig zu ringen,
Wie er durchbräche den Kreis, Willkür zu schaffen den Formen
Wie dem Wollen; doch was er beginnt, beginnt er vergebens.
Denn zwar drängt er sich vor zu diesen Gliedern, zu jenen,
Stattet mächtig sie aus, jedoch schon darben dagegen
Andere Glieder, die Last des Übergewichtes vernichtet
Alle Schöne der Form und alle reine Bewegung.
Siehst du also dem einen Geschöpf besonderen Vorzug
Irgend gegönnt, so frage nur gleich: wo leidet es etwa
Mangel anderswo? und suche mit forschendem Geiste;
Finden wirst du sogleich zu aller Bildung den Schlüssel.
Denn so hat kein Tier, dem sämtliche Zähne den obern
Kiefer umzäunen, ein Horn auf seiner Stirne getragen,
Und daher ist den Löwen gehörnt der ewigen Mutter
Ganz unmöglich zu bilden, und böte sie alle Gewalt auf;
Denn sie hat nicht Masse genug, die Reihen der Zähne
Völlig zu pflanzen und auch Geweih und Hörner zu treiben.

Every animal is an end unto itself; it arises in perfect form
from the womb of nature and engenders perfect children.
All their limbs are formed in accordance with eternal laws,
and even the most unusual shape secretly preserves the original form.
Thus, each mouth is skilled in seizing that food
which is proper for its body; whether its jaws are feeble and toothless,
or armed with powerful teeth, in every case
a well-adapted organ promotes the nourishment of the other parts of the body.
In the same way, every foot, long or short, moves
in complete harmony with the purpose of the animal and its needs.
Thus, for each of her children complete and perfect good health
has been foreordained by its mother: for all living body parts
never contradict each other but all operate to ensure life.
Thus the animal's form determines its way of life,
and the way of life in turn powerfully affects
all forms. Thus the well-ordered development proves to be consistent,
although it is inclined toward change in outwardly operative features.
Yet, inside, the strength of the nobler creatures
is enclosed within the sacred circle of living development.
No god extends these boundaries, nature honors them:
for only when limited this way was perfection ever possible.

But, inside, a spirit seems to be powerfully struggling
for ways to break through the circle, to create free will for the forms
and for the desires; but whatever it undertakes it undertakes in vain.
For, to be sure, it thrusts its way into these body parts or those,
equipping them mightily, but in return other body parts
already atrophy; the burden of the imbalance destroys
all beauty of form and cleanness of movement.
Thus, if you see one creature granted special preference
in any part, ask at once: "Where is it suffering
a lack somewhere else?" and seek this with a probing mind;
you will immediately find the key to all development.
For, in this way, no animal whose upper jaw is fenced
by a complete set of teeth has ever carried a horn on its brow,
and therefore it is totally impossible for the eternal mother
to form a horned lion, even if she summoned up all her power;
for she does not possess enough mass to plant
complete rows of teeth, and to grow antlers and horns as well.

Dieser schöne Begriff von Macht und Schranken, von Willkür
Und Gesetz, von Freiheit und Maß, von beweglicher Ordnung,
Vorzug und Mangel erfreue dich hoch; die heilige Muse
Bringt harmonisch ihn dir, mit sanftem Zwange belehrend.
Keinen höhern Begriff erringt der sittliche Denker,
Keinen der tätige Mann, der dichtende Künstler; der Herrscher,
Der verdient, es zu sein, erfreut nur durch ihn sich der Krone.
Freue dich, höchstes Geschöpf der Natur, du fühlest dich fähig,
Ihr den höchsten Gedanken, zu dem sie schaffend sich aufschwang,
Nachzudenken. Hier stehe nun still und wende die Blicke
Rückwärts, prüfe, vergleiche, und nimm vom Munde der Muse,
Daß du schauest, nicht schwärmst, die liebliche, volle Gewißheit.

## *Schweizerlied*

Ufm Bergli
Bin i gesässe,
Ha de Vögle
Zugeschaut;
Hänt gesunge,
Hänt gesprunge,
Hänt 's Nestli
Gebaut.

In ä Garte
Bin i gestande,
Ha de Imbli
Zugeschaut;
Hänt gebrummet,
Hänt gesummet,
Hänt Zelli
Gebaut.

Uf d' Wiese
Bin i gange,
Lugt i Summer-
Vögle a;
Hänt gesoge,
Hänt gefloge,
Gar z' schön hänt s'
Getan.

Let this beautiful concept of power and limits, of free will
and law, of freedom and measure, of movement within order,
of preferentiality and lack, rejoice you greatly; the holy Muse
brings it to you harmoniously, instructing you with gentle compulsion.
The moral thinker can acquire no higher concept,
nor can the man of action or the literary artist; the ruler
who is worthy to be one enjoys his crown only through that concept.
Rejoice, highest creation of nature, you feel capable
of rethinking in turn the loftiest thought she attained to
while in the act of creating. Now stand still here and turn your eyes
backward; test, compare, and accept from the lips of the Muse—
so that you may truly see, and not idly imagine—precious, complete certainty.

## Swiss Song

On the little hill
I sat,
watching
the birds;
they sang,
they hopped,
they built
their nests.

In a garden
I stood,
watching
the bees;
they hummed,
they buzzed,
they built
their honeycombs.

In the meadow
I walked,
looking at
butterflies;
they sucked nectar,
they flew around,
they did it
really beautifully.

Und da kummt nu
Der Hansel,
Und da zeig i
Em froh,
Wie sie's mache,
Und mer lache
Und mache 's
Au so.

## Der Totentanz

Der Türmer, der schaut zumitten der Nacht
Hinab auf die Gräber in Lage;
Der Mond, der hat alles ins Helle gebracht,
Der Kirchhof, er liegt wie am Tage.
Da regt sich ein Grab und ein anderes dann:
Sie kommen hervor, ein Weib da, ein Mann,
In weißen und schleppenden Hemden.

Das reckt nun, es will sich ergetzen sogleich,
Die Knöchel zur Runde, zum Kranze,
So arm und so jung, und so alt und so reich;
Doch hindern die Schleppen am Tanze.
Und weil hier die Scham nun nicht weiter gebeut,
Sie schütteln sich alle, da liegen zerstreut
Die Hemdelein über den Hügeln.

Nun hebt sich der Schenkel, nun wackelt das Bein,
Gebärden da gibt es vertrackte;
Dann klipperts und klapperts mitunter hinein,
Als schlüg man die Hölzlein zum Takte.
Das kommt nun dem Türmer so lächerlich vor;
Da raunt ihm der Schalk, der Versucher, ins Ohr:
Geh! hole dir einen der Laken.

Getan wie gedacht! und er flüchtet sich schnell
Nun hinter geheiligte Türen.
Der Mond, und noch immer er scheinet so hell
Zum Tanz, den sie schauderlich führen.

And now Hansel
comes along,
and I show
him merrily
how they do it
and we laugh
and do it
the same way.

## The Dance of Death

The watchman in the tower, in the middle of the night he looks
down at the graves all in rows;
the moon has made everything clearly visible;
the churchyard lies there as if in daylight.
Then a grave stirs and, next, another one:
they come out, here a woman, there a man,
in trailing white shrouds.

They want to enjoy themselves at once, and stretch
their ankles in a ring, for a round dance,
both the poor and young, and the old and rich;
but the trailing garments make it hard for them to dance.
And because modesty no longer counts here,
they all shake off their shrouds,
which lie scattered over the grave mounds.

Now the thigh is lifted, now the bone shakes;
contorted gestures are seen there;
then there are occasional clitters and clatters,
as if wooden clappers were being played to the beat.
This now seems so comical to the watchman;
and the scamp, the tempter, whispers in his ear:
"Go get one of the shrouds!"

No sooner thought than done! And now he quickly takes refuge
behind consecrated doors.
The moon still shines brightly
on the dance they perform in such a grisly way.

Doch endlich verlieret sich dieser und der,
Schleicht eins nach dem andern gekleidet einher,
Und husch ist es unter dem Rasen.

Nur einer, der trippelt und stolpert zuletzt
Und tappet und grapst an den Grüften;
Doch hat kein Geselle so schwer ihn verletzt,
Er wittert das Tuch in den Lüften.
Er rüttelt die Turmtür, sie schlägt ihn zurück,
Geziert und gesegnet, dem Türmer zum Glück,
Sie blinkt von metallenen Kreuzen.

Das Hemd muß er haben, da rastet er nicht,
Da gilt auch kein langes Besinnen;
Den gotischen Zierat ergreift nun der Wicht
Und klettert von Zinne zu Zinnen.
Nun ists um den armen, den Türmer getan!
Es ruckt sich von Schnörkel zu Schnörkel hinan,
Langbeinigen Spinnen vergleichbar.

Der Türmer erbleichet, der Türmer erbebt,
Gern gäb er ihn wieder, den Laken.
Da häkelt – jetzt hat er am längsten gelebt –
Den Zipfel ein eiserner Zacken.
Schon trübet der Mond sich, verschwindenden Scheins,
Die Glocke, sie donnert ein mächtiges Eins,
Und unten zerschellt das Gerippe.

## Die wandelnde Glocke

Es war ein Kind, das wollte nie
Zur Kirche sich bequemen,
Und Sonntags fand es stets ein Wie,
Den Weg ins Feld zu nehmen.

Die Mutter sprach: Die Glocke tönt,
Und so ist dirs befohlen,
Und hast du dich nicht hingewöhnt,
Sie kommt und wird dich holen.

But finally this one and that slips away,
one after the other they dress and steal back,
and in a trice they're underneath the turf.

Only one, the last of all, toddles and stumbles
and gropes and grabs at the graves;
but it was none of his companions that did him this great injury,
he scents the cloth up in the air.
He shakes at the tower door, it repels him;
adorned and blessed, to the watchman's good fortune,
it shines with metal crosses.

He must have his shroud, he doesn't stop for rest;
and it's no time to stand around and think;
the fellow now seizes the Gothic ornament
and climbs up from one projection to another.
Now it's all up with the poor watchman!
The dead man moves jerkily from one molding to another,
like a long-legged spider.

The watchman turns pale, the watchman trembles;
he'd gladly return the shroud.
But, as he tries to do so, an iron spike
hooks one corner of the cloth—now his life is at an end.
The moon is already dimming, its shine is disappearing;
the bell thunderously tolls a powerful "One,"
and the skeleton is shattered down below.

## The Walking Bell

There was a child who never would
agree to go to church,
and every Sunday he found some reason
to make his way into the fields.

His mother said: "The bell is ringing,
and so you're commanded to go;
and if you haven't made it a habit,
it will come and get you."

Das Kind, es denkt: Die Glocke hängt
Da droben auf dem Stuhle.
Schon hats den Weg ins Feld gelenkt
Als lief' es aus der Schule.

Die Glocke Glocke tönt nicht mehr,
Die Mutter hat gefackelt.
Doch welch ein Schrecken hinterher!
Die Glocke kommt gewackelt.

Sie wackelt schnell, man glaubt es kaum;
Das arme Kind im Schrecken,
Es lauft, es kommt als wie im Traum;
Die Glocke wird es decken.

Doch nimmt es richtig seinen Husch,
Und mit gewandter Schnelle
Eilt es durch Anger, Feld und Busch
Zur Kirche, zur Kapelle.

Und jeden Sonn- und Feiertag
Gedenkt es an den Schaden,
Läßt durch den ersten Glockenschlag,
Nicht in Person sich laden.

## Gefunden

Ich ging im Walde
So für mich hin,
Und nichts zu suchen,
Das war mein Sinn.

Im Schatten sah ich
Ein Blümchen stehn,
Wie Sterne leuchtend,
Wie Äuglein schön.

Ich wollt es brechen,
Da sagt' es fein:
Soll ich zum Welken
Gebrochen sein?

The child thinks: "The bell is hanging
up there among the roof girders."
He has already turned his steps toward the fields
as if he were running out of school.

'The bell, bell is no longer ringing;
Mother was talking nonsense."
But what a fright behind the child!
The bell comes toddling along.

It toddles quickly, you'd scarcely believe it;
the poor child, terrified,
runs; things are happening as in a dream;
the bell is going to cover him up.

But now the child starts to put on speed,
and with skillful swiftness
he hastens through common, field, and bush
to the church, to the chapel.

And every Sunday and holiday
he remembers that injury,
and lets himself be summoned
by the first sound of the bell; no one needs to speak to him.

## Found

I was walking in the woods
aimlessly,
and had no intention
of looking for anything.

In the shade I saw
a little flower standing,
shining like stars,
beautiful as girls' eyes.

I wanted to pick it,
when it said sweetly:
"Am I to be picked
so I'll wither?"

Ich grubs mit allen
Den Würzlein aus,
Zum Garten trug ichs
Am hübschen Haus.

Und pflanzt es wieder
Am stillen Ort;
Nun zweigt es immer
Und blüht so fort.

## *Ballade*

Herein, o du Guter! du Alter, herein!
Hier unten im Saale, da sind wir allein,
Wir wollen die Pforte verschließen.
Die Mutter, sie betet; der Vater im Hain
Ist gangen, die Wölfe zu schießen.
O sing uns ein Märchen, o sing es uns oft,
Daß ich und der Bruder es lerne;
Wir haben schon längst einen Sänger gehofft –
Die Kinder, sie hören es gerne.

Im nächtlichen Schrecken, im feindlichen Graus
Verläßt er das hohe, das herrliche Haus,
Die Schätze, die hat er vergraben.
Der Graf nun so eilig zum Pförtchen hinaus,
Was mag er im Arme denn haben?
Was birget er unter dem Mantel geschwind?
Was trägt er so rasch in die Ferne?
Ein Töchterlein ist es, da schläft nun das Kind –
Die Kinder, sie hören es gerne.

Nun hellt sich der Morgen, die Welt ist so weit,
In Tälern und Wäldern die Wohnung bereit,
In Dörfern erquickt man den Sänger.
So schreitet und heischt er undenkliche Zeit,
Der Bart wächst ihm länger und länger;
Doch wächst in dem Arme das liebliche Kind,
Wie unter dem glücklichsten Sterne,

I dug it out
with all its little roots,
and carried it to the garden
by my pretty house.

And replanted it
in a quiet place;
now it keeps putting out sprigs
and continues to bloom there.

## Ballad

"Come in, good man! Old man, come in!
Down here in the great hall we'll be alone,
we'll lock the door.
Mother is praying; Father has gone
to the woods to shoot wolves.
Oh, sing us a tale, sing it over and over for us,
so my brother and I can learn it;
for a long time now we've been hoping for a minstrel."
The children listen with pleasure.

"In the terror of night, in the hostile dread,
he leaves behind his lofty, splendid house;
he has buried his treasures.
The count, now hastening so out of his wicket,
what is it he has in his arms?
What is he concealing beneath his cloak as he quickly goes?
What is he carrying far away so swiftly?
It's a little daughter, the child is now asleep."
The children listen with pleasure.

"Now the morning grows bright, the world is so wide,
a dwelling is ready in valleys and forests;
people refresh the minstrel in the villages.
And so he walks and asks for food for an unimaginably long time,
his beard growing longer and longer;
but the lovely child grows in his arms,
as if beneath the luckiest of stars,

Geschützt in dem Mantel vor Regen und Wind –
Die Kinder, sie hören es gerne.

Und immer sind weiter die Jahre gerückt,
Der Mantel entfärbt sich, der Mantel zerstückt,
Er könnte sie länger nicht fassen.
Der Vater, er schaut sie, wie ist er beglückt!
Er kann sich für Freude nicht lassen;
So schön und so edel erscheint sie zugleich,
Entsprossen aus tüchtigem Kerne,
Wie macht sie den Vater, den teuren, so reich –
Die Kinder, sie hören es gerne.

Da reitet ein fürstlicher Ritter heran,
Sie recket die Hand aus, der Gabe zu nahn;
Almosen will er nicht geben.
Er fasset das Händchen so kräftiglich an:
Die will ich, so ruft er, aufs Leben!
Erkennst du, erwidert der Alte, den Schatz,
Erhebst du zur Fürstin sie gerne;
Sie sei dir verlobet auf grünendem Platz –
Die Kinder, sie hören es gerne.

Sie segnet der Priester am heiligen Ort;
Mit Lust und mit Unlust nun ziehet sie fort,
Sie möchte vom Vater nicht scheiden.
Der Alte, er wandelt nun hier und bald dort,
Er träget in Freuden sein Leiden.
So hab ich mir Jahre die Tochter gedacht,
Die Enkelein wohl in der Ferne;
Sie segn ich bei Tage, sie segn ich bei Nacht –
Die Kinder, sie hören es gerne.

Er segnet die Kinder; da polterts am Tor,
Der Vater, da ist er! Sie springen hervor,
Sie können den Alten nicht bergen –
Was lockst du die Kinder! du Bettler! du Tor!
Ergreift ihn, ihr eisernen Schergen!
Zum tiefsten Verlies den Verwegenen fort!
Die Mutter vernimmts in der Ferne,

protected from rain and wind in his cloak."
The children listen with pleasure.

"And the years have moved on and on;
the cloak is faded, the cloak is in shreds,
it would no longer be able to contain her.
The father, looking at her, how happy he is!
He's beside himself with joy;
she looks so beautiful and so noble at the same time,
sprouted from an excellent seed;
how rich she makes her dear father!"
The children listen with pleasure.

"Then a princely knight rides by;
she stretches out her hand to bring it nearer to his gift,
but he refuses to give alms.
He seizes her little hand with such force:
'I want her for all my life!' he cries.
The old man replies, 'If you realize what a treasure she is,
you will gladly raise her to the rank of princess;
let her be betrothed to you on the green square.'"
The children listen with pleasure.

"The priest blesses them in the holy place;
with pleasure and displeasure she now goes away;
she doesn't like parting with her father.
The old man wanders now here, now there,
bearing his sorrows in the midst of his joy.
Thus I have pictured my daughter for years,
and my grandchildren, I suppose, far away;
I bless them by day, I bless them by night."
The children listen with pleasure.

He blesses the children; then there's a racket at the door.
Their father is here! They leap in front of the old man,
but cannot conceal him.
"Why are you luring my children, you beggar, you fool?
Seize him, you ironclad bailiffs!
Carry out this rash man to the deepest dungeon!"
Their mother hears this from the distance;

Sie eilet, sie bittet mit schmeichelndem Wort—
Die Kinder, sie hören es gerne.

Die Schergen, sie lassen den Würdigen stehn,
Und Mutter und Kinder, sie bitten so schön;
Der fürstliche Stolze verbeißet
Die grimmige Wut, ihn entrüstet das Flehn,
Bis endlich sein Schweigen zerreißet:
Du niedrige Brut! du vom Bettlergeschlecht!
Verfinsterung fürstlicher Sterne!
Ihr bringt mir Verderben! Geschieht mir doch recht—
Die Kinder, sie hörens nicht gerne.

Noch stehet der Alte mit herrlichem Blick,
Die eisernen Schergen, sie treten zurück,
Es wächst nur das Toben und Wüten.
Schon lange verflucht ich mein ehliches Glück,
Das sind nun die Früchte der Blüten!
Man leugnete stets, und man leugnet mit Recht,
Daß je sich der Adel erlerne;
Die Bettlerin zeugte mir Bettlergeschlecht—
Die Kinder, sie hörens nicht gerne.

Und wenn euch der Gatte, der Vater verstößt,
Die heiligsten Bande verwegentlich löst,
So kommt zu dem Vater, dem Ahnen!
Der Bettler vermag, so ergraut und entblößt,
Euch herrliche Wege zu bahnen.
Die Burg, die ist meine! Du hast sie geraubt,
Mich trieb dein Geschlecht in die Ferne;
Wohl bin ich mit köstlichen Siegeln beglaubt!—
Die Kinder, sie hören es gerne.

Rechtmäßiger König, er kehret zurück,
Den Treuen verleiht er entwendetes Glück,
Ich löse die Siegel der Schätze.—
So rufet der Alte mit freundlichem Blick:
Euch künd ich die milden Gesetze.
Erhole dich, Sohn! Es entwickelt sich gut,
Heut einen sich selige Sterne;
Die Fürstin, sie zeugte dir fürstliches Blut—
Die Kinder, sie hören es gerne.

she rushes in, beseeching him with flattering words.
The children listen with pleasure.

The bailiffs leave the worthy man alone,
and mother and children intercede for him so beautifully;
the prideful prince suppresses
his fierce anger, he is indignant at their beseeching
until his silence finally ends violently:
"You low creature, child of a line of beggars!
You cast a dark shadow over my princely stars!
All of you bring me ruin! But it serves me right!"
The children listen with displeasure.

The old man still stands there with a masterful look;
the ironclad bailiffs retreat;
the ranting and raving merely increase.
"For a long time now I have cursed my marital happiness,
now these are the fruits from the blossoms!
It has always been denied, and rightly denied,
that nobility can ever be learned;
the beggar woman produced a family of beggars for me!"
The children listen with displeasure.

"And even if you are rejected by your husband and father,
who rashly breaks the most sacred bonds,
then come to your father and grandfather!
As gray and destitute as he may be, the beggar is able
to blaze splendid trails for you.
The castle is mine! You stole it;
Your family drove me into distant exile;
but I have precious seals to verify my claims!"
The children listen with pleasure.

"The rightful king returns,
he restores their purloined happiness to those who remained faithful;
I break the seals of my treasures."
Thus calls the old man, with friendliness in his eyes:
"I announce lenient laws for you.
Come to yourself, son! Things are taking a good turn,
today favorable stars are in conjunction;
the princess gave birth to princely blood."
The children listen with pleasure.

## Kriegsglück

Verwünschter weiß ich nichts im Krieg,
Als nicht blessiert zu sein.
Man geht getrost von Sieg zu Sieg
Gefahrgewohnt hinein;
Hat abgepackt und aufgepackt
Und weiter nichts ereilt,
Als daß man auf dem Marsch sich plackt,
Im Lager langeweilt.

Dann geht das Kantonieren an,
Dem Bauer eine Last,
Verdrießlich jedem Edelmann,
Und Bürgern gar verhaßt.
Sei höflich, man bedient dich schlecht,
Den Grobian zur Not;
Und nimmt man selbst am Wirte Recht,
Ißt man Profossen-Brot.

Wenn endlich die Kanone brummt
Und knattert 's klein Gewehr,
Trompet und Trab und Trommel summt,
Da gehts wohl lustig her;
Und wie nun das Gefecht befiehlt,
Man weichet, man erneuts,
Man retiriert, man avanciert –
Und immer ohne Kreuz.

Nun endlich pfeift Musketen-Blei
Und trifft, wills Gott, das Bein,
Und nun ist alle Not vorbei,
Man schleppt uns gleich hinein
Zum Städtchen, das der Sieger deckt,
Wohin man grimmig kam;
Die Frauen, die man erst erschreckt,
Sind liebenswürdig zahm.

Da tut sich Herz und Keller los,
Die Küche darf nicht ruhn;
Auf weicher Betten Flaumen-Schoß
Kann man sich gütlich tun.

## *Fortunes of War*

I know of nothing more accursed in war
than not to be wounded.
You go confidently from one victory to another,
accustomed to danger;
you've packed your belongings and loaded them
and accomplished nothing more
than fatiguing yourself on the march
and being bored in camp.

Then the quartering begins,
a burden for the peasant,
an annoyance to every nobleman,
and really hateful to townsfolk.
If you're polite, you're badly served;
in an emergency, play the roughneck;
and if you stick up for your rights with your host,
you wind up eating guardhouse bread.

When the cannon finally roars
and small arms rattle,
when trumpet, trot, and drum are sounding,
that, yes, is a merry time;
and accordingly as the battle demands,
you pull back, you charge again,
you retreat, you advance —
and always without winning a medal.

Now musket lead is finally whistling
and, God willing, hits you in the leg,
and now all the distress is over;
they drag you right into
the town that the victor is holding,
the same one you arrived at in anger.
The women you scared at first
are now tame and friendly.

Then hearts and wine cellars open up,
and they won't let the kitchen rest;
you can be comfortable
in the downy lap of soft beds.

Der kleine Flügelbube hupft,
Die Wirtin rastet nie,
Sogar das Hemdchen wird zerzupft,
Das nenn ich doch Scharpie!

Hat eine sich den Helden nun
Beinah herangepflegt,
So kann die Nachbarin nicht ruhn,
Die ihn gesellig hegt.
Ein Drittes kommt wohl emsiglich,
Am Ende fehlet keins,
Und in der Mitte sieht er sich
Des sämtlichen Vereins.

Der König hört von guter Hand,
Man sei voll Kampfes-Lust;
Da kömmt behende Kreuz und Band
Und zieret Rock und Brust.
Sagt, obs für einen Martismann
Wohl etwas Beßres gibt!
Und unter Tränen scheidet man,
Geehrt so wie geliebt.

## Elemente

Aus wie vielen Elementen
Soll ein echtes Lied sich nähren,
Daß es Laien gern empfinden,
Meister es mit Freuden hören?

Liebe sei vor allen Dingen
Unser Thema, wenn wir singen;
Kann sie gar das Lied durchdringen,
Wirds um desto besser klingen.

Dann muß Klang der Gläser tönen
Und Rubin des Weins erglänzen:
Denn für Liebende, für Trinker
Winkt man mit den schönsten Kränzen.

The little boy with wings hops around,
your hostess never relaxes;
even her shift gets plucked to bits:
that's what I call bandage lint!

If one of the ladies has now
tended her hero nearly to the point of recovery,
her neighbor can't rest:
she must entertain him socially.
A third one comes along busily,
finally none of them is missing;
and he finds himself in the midst
of the entire circle.

The king hears on good authority
that you're full of eagerness for battle;
then the medal and ribbon come quickly
to adorn your jacket and breast.
Tell me whether there's anything better
for a follower of Mars!
And there are tears when you say good-bye,
you're honored as well as loved.

## Elements

From how many elements
should a genuine song be nourished
so laymen will gladly accept it
and masters will hear it with joy?

Above all else, let love
be our theme when we sing;
if it can even permeate the song,
it will sound all the better.

Then, the clink of glasses must be heard
and the ruby of wine must shine:
because for lovers, for drinkers,
people beckon with the most beautiful wreaths.

Waffenklang wird auch gefodert,
Daß auch die Drommete schmettre;
Daß, wenn Glück zu Flammen lodert,
Sich im Sieg der Held vergöttre.

Dann zuletzt ist unerläßlich,
Daß der Dichter manches hasse;
Was unleidlich ist und häßlich,
Nicht wie Schönes leben lasse.

Weiß der Sänger, dieser viere
Urgewaltgen Stoff zu mischen,
Hafis gleich wird er die Völker
Ewig freuen und erfrischen.

## Phänomen

Wenn zu der Regenwand
Phöbus sich gattet,
Gleich steht ein Bogenrand
Farbig beschattet.

Im Nebel gleichen Kreis
Seh ich gezogen;
Zwar ist der Bogen weiß,
Doch Himmelsbogen.

So sollst du, muntrer Greis,
Dich nicht betrüben;
Sind gleich die Haare weiß,
Doch wirst du lieben.

## "Solang man nüchtern ist"

Solang man nüchtern ist,
Gefällt das Schlechte;
Wie man getrunken hat,
Weiß man das Rechte;

The clash of weapons is also in demand,
so that the trumpet should clang as well;
so that, when happiness flares up into flames,
the hero will be deified in victory.

Then, finally, it is obligatory
for the poet to have many hates;
he should not let unpleasant and ugly things
flourish as if they were beautiful.

If the singer knows how to mix
the all-powerful material of these four things,
like Hafiz he will eternally
rejoice and refresh all nations.

## Phenomenon

When Phoebus mingles
with the wall of rain,
immediately the edge of a bow appears,
shaded into colors.

In the mist I see
a similar arc drawn;
to be sure, the bow is white,
but still a heavenly bow.

And so, sprightly old man,
you should not be gloomy;
even if your hair is white,
still you'll fall in love.

## *"All the time a man is sober"*

All the time a man is sober,
he's pleased with inferior things;
as soon as he's had a drink,
he knows what's right;

Nur ist das Übermaß
Auch gleich zuhanden:
Hafis, o lehre mich,
Wie du's verstanden!

Denn meine Meinung ist
Nicht übertrieben:
Wenn man nicht trinken kann,
Soll man nicht lieben;
Doch sollt ihr Trinker euch
Nicht besser dünken:
Wenn man nicht lieben kann,
Soll man nicht trinken.

## Selige Sehnsucht

Sagt es niemand, nur den Weisen,
Weil die Menge gleich verhöhnet,
Das Lebendge will ich preisen,
Das nach Flammentod sich sehnet.

In der Liebesnächte Kühlung,
Die dich zeugte, wo du zeugtest,
Überfällt dich fremde Fühlung,
Wenn die stille Kerze leuchtet.

Nicht mehr bleibest du umfangen
In der Finsternis Beschattung,
Und dich reißet neu Verlangen
Auf zu höherer Begattung.

Keine Ferne macht dich schwierig,
Kommst geflogen und gebannt,
Und zuletzt, des Lichts begierig,
Bist du, Schmetterling, verbrannt.

Und solang du das nicht hast,
Dieses: Stirb und werde!
Bist du nur ein trüber Gast
Auf der dunklen Erde.

only, it's all too easy
to overdo it:
Hafiz, teach me
how you managed it!

Because my opinion
is no exaggeration:
if you can't drink,
you shouldn't love;
but you drinkers shouldn't
feel superior:
if you can't love,
you shouldn't drink.

## Blissful Longing

Tell nobody except the wise,
because the mob is immediately scornful;
I wish to praise that element of life
which longs for a fiery death.

In that coolness of nights of love
Which begat you, where you begat,
an unfamiliar sensation comes over you
when the silent taper shines.

No longer do you remain embraced
by the shadow of the darkness,
but a new desire draws you
upward to a higher form of mating.

No degree of distance makes you doubtful;
you fly over and fall under a spell,
and, at last, lusting for the light,
like a moth you are burned to death.

And so long as you don't have it,
this "Die and be transformed!,"
you will only be a gloomy guest
on the dark earth.

## Schenke

Nennen dich den großen Dichter,
Wenn dich auf dem Markte zeigest;
Gerne hör ich, wenn du singest,
Und ich horche, wenn du schweigest.

Doch ich liebe dich noch lieber,
Wenn du küssest zum Erinnern;
Denn die Worte gehn vorüber,
Und der Kuß, der bleibt im Innern.

Reim auf Reim will was bedeuten,
Besser ist es, viel zu denken.
Singe du den andern Leuten
Und verstumme mit dem Schenken.

## Siebenschläfer

Sechs Begünstigte des Hofes
Fliehen vor des Kaisers Grimme,
Der als Gott sich läßt verehren,
Doch als Gott sich nicht bewähret:
Denn ihn hindert eine Fliege,
Guter Bissen sich zu freuen.
Seine Diener scheuchen wedelnd,
Nicht verjagen sie die Fliege.
Sie umschwärmt ihn, sticht und irret
Und verwirrt die ganze Tafel,
Kehret wieder wie des hämschen
Fliegengottes Abgesandter.

Nun – so sagen sich die Knaben –
Sollt ein Flieglein Gott verhindern?
Sollt ein Gott auch trinken, speisen,
Wie wir andern? Nein, der Eine,
Der die Sonn erschuf, den Mond auch,
Und der Sterne Glut uns wölbte,

## Cupbearer

They call you the great poet
when you appear in the market;
I like to hear you sing,
and I listen when you're silent.

But I love you even more
when you kiss me for remembrance' sake;
because words pass away
but the kiss remains inside me.

Rhyme upon rhyme is surely significant,
but it's better to think a lot.
So sing to other people
and be silent with your cupbearer.

## The Seven Sleepers

Six court favorites
flee the wrath of the emperor,
who wishes to be revered as a god,
but doesn't prove himself to be a god:
for a fly prevents him
from enjoying his fine meal.
His servants try to scare it away with whisks,
but cannot chase away the fly.
It circles around him, bites him, and roams about,
and sets the whole banquet in confusion,
always returning like an envoy
of the malicious Lord of Flies.

"Now," say the lads,
"should a little fly thwart a god?
Should a god also drink and eat
like the rest of us? No, the One
who created the sun and also the moon
and arched the heat of the stars over our head,

Dieser ists, wir fliehn! – Die zarten,
Leicht beschuht-, beputzten Knaben
Nimmt ein Schäfer auf, verbirgt sie
Und sich selbst in Felsenhöhle.
Schäfershund, er will nicht weichen,
Weggescheucht, den Fuß zerschmettert,
Drängt er sich an seinen Herren
Und gesellt sich zum Verborgnen,
Zu den Lieblingen des Schlafes.

Und der Fürst, dem sie entflohen,
Liebentrüstet, sinnt auf Strafen,
Weiset ab so Schwert als Feuer,
In die Höhle sie mit Ziegeln
Und mit Kalk sie läßt vermauern.

Aber jene schlafen immer,
Und der Engel, ihr Beschützer,
Sagt vor Gottes Thron berichtend:
So zur Rechten, so zur Linken
Hab ich immer sie gewendet,
Daß die schönen jungen Glieder
Nicht des Moders Qualm verletze.
Spalten riß ich in die Felsen,
Daß die Sonne, steigend, sinkend,
Junge Wangen frisch erneute:
Und so liegen sie beseligt.
Auch, auf heilen Vorderpfoten,
Schläft das Hündlein süßen Schlummers.

Jahre fliehen, Jahre kommen,
Wachen endlich auf die Knaben,
Und die Mauer, die vermorschte,
Altershalben ist gefallen.
Und Jamblika sagt, der Schöne,
Ausgebildete vor allen,
Als der Schäfer fürchtend zaudert:
Lauf ich hin! und hol euch Speise,
Leben wag ich und das Goldstück!

it is only He. Let's run away!" The tender lads,
wearing light shoes and garments,
are given shelter by a shepherd, who conceals them
and himself in a cave among the cliffs.
The shepherd's dog refuses to leave;
though driven away and suffering a broken paw,
he presses up against his master
and joins the number of the concealed ones,
the favorites of sleep.

And the monarch from whom they have run away,
furious with rebuked love, plans punishments
but refuses to do so by sword or fire;
he has them walled up in the cave
with bricks and mortar.

But they sleep on,
and the angel, their guardian,
says in his report before the throne of God:
"I have continued to turn them,
now to the right, now to the left,
so that their handsome young limbs
are not injured by the gases of corruption.
I tore cracks into the rocks,
so that the sun, rising and setting,
can keep their young cheeks fresh and new:
and so they lie in a state of bliss.
Also, the little dog is sleeping
a sweet sleep, with healed forepaws."

Years fly by, years arrive;
the lads finally awaken,
and the decayed masonry
has fallen with age.
And handsome Jamblika,
the best-educated of them all, says,
when the shepherd fearfully hesitates:
"I'll run out and bring you food;
I'll risk my life and this gold piece!"

Ephesus, gar manches Jahr schon,
Ehrt die Lehre des Propheten
Jesus. (Friede sei dem Guten!)

Und er lief. Da war der Tore
Wart und Turn und alles anders.
Doch zum nächsten Bäckerladen
Wandt er sich nach Brot in Eile.
Schelm! so rief der Bäcker, hast du,
Jüngling, einen Schatz gefunden!
Gib mir, dich verrät das Goldstück,
Mir die Hälfte zum Versöhnen!

Und sie hadern.–Vor den König
Kommt der Handel; auch der König
Will nur teilen wie der Bäcker.

Nun betätigt sich das Wunder
Nach und nach aus hundert Zeichen.
An dem selbsterbauten Palast
Weiß er sich sein Recht zu sichern.
Denn ein Pfeiler, durchgegraben,
Führt zu scharfbenamsten Schätzen.
Gleich versammeln sich Geschlechter
Ihre Sippschaft zu beweisen.
Und als Ururvater prangend
Steht Jamblikas Jugendfülle.
Wie von Ahnherrn hört er sprechen
Hier von seinem Sohn und Enkeln;
Der Urenkel Schar umgibt ihn,
Als ein Volk von tapfern Männern,
Ihn, den Jüngsten, zu verehren.
Und ein Merkmal übers andre
Dringt sich auf, Beweis vollendend;
Sich und den Gefährten hat er
Die Persönlichkeit bestätigt.

Nun zur Höhle kehrt er wieder,
Volk und König ihn geleiten.–
Nicht zum König, nicht zum Volke
Kehrt der Auserwählte wieder:

Ephesus for many a year now
has revered the religion of the Prophet
Jesus (peace be on the good Prophet!).

And he ran out. There he saw the watchmen
and towers at the gates, and all the rest.
But he swiftly turned toward the nearest
bakery for bread.
"Rascal!" the baker cried. "So,
young man, you've found a hidden treasure!
The gold coin betrays you; give me
half to keep me quiet!"

And they bicker. The story
reaches the king; and the king, too,
wants nothing else than to have his share, like the baker.

Now the miracle is confirmed
gradually, from a hundred bits of evidence.
He is able to authenticate his claim
by means of the palace he himself once built:
for a pillar, when dug through,
leads to accurately described treasures.
At once relatives assemble
to give proof of their kinship,
and Jamblika, in the bloom of youth, stands
there resplendently as a great-great-grandfather.
Here he hears talk of his son and grandchildren
as if they were grandfathers;
a crowd of his own great-grandchildren surrounds him,
like a nation of brave men,
to honor him, the youngest of them all.
And one identifying sign after another
comes to light, completing the proof;
he has established the identity
of himself and his companions.

Now he returns to the cave,
accompanied by the people and the king.—
But the chosen one never returns
to the king or to the people;

Denn die Sieben, die von lang her,
Achte warens mit dem Hunde,
Sich von aller Welt gesondert,
Gabriels geheim Vermögen
Hat, gemäß dem Willen Gottes,
Sie dem Paradies geeignet,
Und die Höhle schien vermauert.

## "In tausend Formen magst du dich verstecken"

In tausend Formen magst du dich verstecken,
Doch, Allerliebste, gleich erkenn ich dich;
Du magst mit Zauberschleiern dich bedecken,
Allgegenwärtge, gleich erkenn ich dich.

An der Zypresse reinstem, jungem Streben,
Allschöngewachsne, gleich erkenn ich dich;
In des Kanales reinem Wellenleben,
Allschmeichelhafte, wohl erkenn ich dich.

Wenn steigend sich der Wasserstrahl entfaltet,
Allspielende, wie froh erkenn ich dich;
Wenn Wolke sich gestaltend umgestaltet,
Allmannigfaltge, dort erkenn ich dich.

An des geblümten Schleiers Wiesenteppich,
Allbuntbesternte, schön erkenn ich dich;
Und greift umher ein tausendarmger Eppich,
O Allumklammernde, da kenn ich dich.

Wenn am Gebirg der Morgen sich entzündet,
Gleich, Allerheiternde, begrüß ich dich;
Dann über mir der Himmel rein sich ründet,
Allherzerweiternde, dann atm ich dich.

Was ich mit äußerm Sinn, mit innerm kenne,
Du Allbelehrende, kenn ich durch dich;
Und wenn ich Allahs Namenhundert nenne,
Mit jedem klingt ein Name nach für dich.

for the seven, who long ago
(they were eight counting the dog)
were separated from the whole world,
have been, by Gabriel's mysterious power
and in accordance with the will of God,
appropriated for Paradise,
and the cave seemed to be walled up again.

## *"You may conceal yourself in a thousand forms"*

You may conceal yourself in a thousand forms,
but, all-beloved one, I recognize you at once;
you may cover yourself with magic veils,
all-present one, I recognize you at once.

In the purest youthful striving of the cypress,
all-shapely one, I recognize you at once;
in the pure watery life of the canal,
all-flattering one, I surely recognize you.

When a jet of water rises and unfurls,
all-sportive one, how happily I recognize you;
when a cloud, forming shapes, changes shape,
all-manifold one, there I recognize you.

In the meadowy tapestry of the flowered veil,
all-motley-starred one, I recognize your beauty;
and if a thousand-armed ivy gropes about,
O all-embracing one, there I know you.

When the morning ignites itself against the mountain,
at once, all-cheering one, I greet you;
then the sky forms a pure dome above me,
all-heart-expanding one, then I breathe you in.

What I know with my outer, with my inner senses,
you all-instructing one, I know through you;
and when I recite Allah's hundred names,
with each one a name reechoes for you.

## Lied und Gebilde

Mag der Grieche seinen Ton
Zu Gestalten drücken,
An der eignen Hände Sohn
Steigern sein Entzücken;

Aber uns ist wonnereich,
In den Euphrat greifen
Und im flüßgen Element
Hin und wider schweifen.

Löscht ich so der Seele Brand,
Lied, es wird erschallen;
Schöpft des Dichters reine Hand,
Wasser wird sich ballen.

## Hatem

Nicht Gelegenheit macht Diebe,
Sie ist selbst der größte Dieb;
Denn sie stahl den Rest der Liebe,
Die mir noch im Herzen blieb.

Dir hat sie ihn übergeben,
Meines Lebens Vollgewinn,
Daß ich nun, verarmt, mein Leben
Nur von dir gewärtig bin.

Doch ich fühle schon Erbarmen
Im Karfunkel deines Blicks
Und erfreu in deinen Armen
Mich erneuerten Geschicks.

## Song and Formation

Let the Greek press
his clay into shapes,
enhancing his delight
in the son of his own hands;

but for us it is rapturous
to put our hands into the Euphrates
and roam back and forth
in the liquid element.

Once I have thus quenched the blaze in my soul,
a song will resound;
when the poet's pure hand creates,
water will become solid.

## Hatem

It's not Opportunity that makes the thief,
she herself is the greatest thief,
for she stole all the love
that was still left in my heart.

She handed it over to you,
all the earnings of my whole life,
so that now, impoverished, I can expect
to receive life only from you.

But I already sense pity
in the garnet of your eyes
and in your arms I rejoice
in a renewal of my destiny.

## Suleika

Hochbeglückt in deiner Liebe
Schelt ich nicht Gelegenheit;
Ward sie auch an dir zum Diebe,
Wie mich solch ein Raub erfreut!

Und wozu denn auch berauben?
Gib dich mir aus freier Wahl;
Gar zu gerne möcht ich glauben –
Ja, ich bins, die dich bestahl.

Was so willig du gegeben,
Bringt dir herrlichen Gewinn;
Meine Ruh, mein reiches Leben
Geb ich freudig, nimm es hin!

Scherze nicht! Nichts von Verarmen!
Macht uns nicht die Liebe reich?
Halt ich dich in meinen Armen,
Jedem Glück ist meines gleich.

## "Als ich auf dem Euphrat schiffte"

SULEIKA. Als ich auf dem Euphrat schiffte,
Streifte sich der goldne Ring
Fingerab in Wasserklüfte,
Den ich jüngst von dir empfing.

Also träumt ich. Morgenröte
Blitzt ins Auge durch den Baum.
Sag, Poete, sag, Prophete!
Was bedeutet dieser Traum?

HATEM. Dies zu deuten bin erbötig!
Hab ich dir nicht oft erzählt,
Wie der Doge von Venedig
Mit dem Meere sich vermählt?

## Suleika

Profoundly happy in your love,
I don't upbraid Opportunity;
even if she played the thief with you,
how a theft like that gladdens me!

And, then, why speak of stealing at all?
Give yourself to me of your own free choice;
all too gladly I would believe—
yes, I'm the one who robbed you.

What you gave away so willingly
will bring you a splendid profit;
I gladly give you my peace of mind,
my rich life—take them!

Don't joke! Say nothing about impoverishment!
Doesn't love make us wealthy?
When I hold you in my arms,
my good fortune is equal to anyone's.

## *"As I was boating on the Euphrates"*

SULEIKA: As I was boating on the Euphrates,
the golden ring
I recently received from you
slipped off my finger into watery chasms.

That was my dream. Dawn
flashes into my eyes through the trees.
Tell me, poet, tell me, prophet!
What does this dream mean?

HATEM: To interpret it, I'm at your service!
Haven't I often told you
how the Doge of Venice
is married to the sea?

So von deinen Fingergliedern
Fiel der Ring dem Euphrat zu.
Ach, zu tausend Himmelsliedern,
Süßer Traum, begeisterst du!

Mich, der von den Indostanen
Streifte bis Damaskus hin,
Um mit neuen Karawanen
Bis ans Rote Meer zu ziehn,

Mich vermählst du deinem Flusse,
Der Terrasse, diesem Hain;
Hier soll bis zum letzten Kusse
Dir mein Geist gewidmet sein.

## *Suleika*

Was bedeutet die Bewegung?
Bringt der Ost mir frohe Kunde?
Seiner Schwingen frische Regung
Kühlt des Herzens tiefe Wunde.

Kosend spielt er mit dem Staube,
Jagt ihn auf in leichten Wölkchen,
Treibt zur sichern Rebenlaube
Der Insekten frohes Völkchen.

Lindert sanft der Sonne Glühen,
Kühlt auch mir die heißen Wangen,
Küßt die Reben noch im Fliehen,
Die auf Feld und Hügel prangen.

Und mir bringt sein leises Flüstern
Von dem Freunde tausend Grüße;
Eh noch diese Hügel düstern,
Grüßen mich wohl tausend Küsse.

In the same way, the ring fell
from your finger joints into the Euphrates.
Ah, sweet dream, you inspire
a thousand heavenly songs!

I, who have roamed from Hindustan
all the way to Damascus,
in order to travel to the Red Sea
with new caravans,

it is I whom you wed to your river,
to its terraced banks, to this grove;
here, until my final kiss,
my mind shall be dedicated to you.

## Suleika

What's the meaning of this agitation?
Is the east wind bringing me happy news?
The fresh beating of its wings
cools my heart's deep wound.

Caressingly it plays with the dust,
chasing it up in light puffs of cloud;
it drives the merry insect folk
to seek safety in the vine leaves.

It gently relieves the sun's heat,
cooling my hot cheeks, too;
in the act of passing by, it kisses the grapevines
that stand resplendent on field and hill.

And its soft whisper brings me
a thousand greetings from my friend;
even before these hills grow dim,
I am greeted by at least a thousand kisses.

Und so kannst du weiter ziehen!
Diene Freunden und Betrübten.
Dort, wo hohe Mauern glühen,
Find ich bald den Vielgeliebten.

Ach, die wahre Herzenskunde,
Liebeshauch, erfrischtes Leben
Wird mir nur aus seinem Munde,
Kann mir nur sein Atem geben.

## Hatem

Locken, haltet mich gefangen
In dem Kreise des Gesichts!
Euch geliebten, braunen Schlangen
Zu erwidern hab ich nichts.

Nur dies Herz, es ist von Dauer,
Schwillt in jugendlichstem Flor;
Unter Schnee und Nebelschauer
Rast ein Ätna dir hervor.

Du beschämst wie Morgenröte
Jener Gipfel ernste Wand,
Und noch einmal fühlet Hatem
Frühlingshauch und Sommerbrand.

Schenke her! Noch eine Flasche!
Diesen Becher bring ich ihr!
Findet sie ein Häufchen Asche,
Sagt sie: Der verbrannte mir.

## Lust und Qual

Knabe saß ich, Fischerknabe,
Auf dem schwarzen Fels im Meer,
Und, bereitend falsche Gabe,
Sang ich, lauschend ringsumher.

And so, you can travel on!
Be of service to friends and sad people.
There where high walls are gleaming
I shall soon find the man I love so dearly.

Ah, the true news from the heart,
the breeze of love, renewed life,
I shall receive only from his lips,
only his breath can give me that.

## Hatem

Tresses, hold me spellbound
within the circle of her face!
I have nothing worthy to offer in return
for you, beloved brown serpents.

Only this heart is constant,
surging in the very flower of youth;
beneath the snow and misty shower
an Etna erupts for you.

Like dawn, you put to shame
the solemn wall of yonder mountain peaks,
and once again Hatem feels
the breath of spring and the blaze of summer.

Cupbearer, here! Another bottle!
I drink this goblet to her!
If she finds a small heap of ashes,
she'll say: "He burned up for me."

## Pleasure and Torment

A lad, a fisher lad, I sat
on the black rock in the sea,
and, preparing deceptive gifts,
I sang, listening to everything around me.

Angel schwebte lockend nieder;
Gleich ein Fischlein streift und schnappt,
Schadenfrohe Schelmenlieder –
Und das Fischlein war ertappt.

Ach! am Ufer, durch die Fluren,
Ins Geklüfte tief zum Hain,
Folgt ich einer Sohle Spuren,
Und die Hirtin war allein.
Blicke sinken, Worte stocken! –
Wie ein Taschenmesser schnappt,
Faßte sie mich in die Locken,
Und das Bübchen war ertappt.

Weiß doch Gott, mit welchem Hirten
Sie aufs neue sich ergeht!
Muß ich in das Meer mich gürten,
Wie es sauset, wie es weht.
Wenn mich oft im Netze jammert
Das Gewimmel groß und klein,
Immer möcht ich noch umklammert
Noch von ihren Armen sein!

## Prooemion

Im Namen dessen, der sich selbst erschuf!
Von Ewigkeit in schaffendem Beruf;
In seinem Namen, der den Glauben schafft,
Vertrauen, Liebe, Tätigkeit und Kraft;
In jenes Namen, der, so oft genannt,
Dem Wesen nach blieb immer unbekannt:

So weit das Ohr, so weit das Auge reicht,
Du findest nur Bekanntes, das ihm gleicht,
Und deines Geistes höchster Feuerflug
Hat schon am Gleichnis, hat am Bild genug;
Es zieht dich an, es reißt dich heiter fort,
Und wo du wandelst, schmückt sich Weg und Ort;
Du zählst nicht mehr, berechnest keine Zeit,
Und jeder Schritt ist Unermeßlichkeit.

My line floated down alluringly;
at once a little fish darted up and bit;
roguish songs delighting in its misery—
and the little fish was caught.

Ah, on shore, across the meadows,
into the chasm down to the grove,
. followed the track of a pair of shoes,
and found the shepherdess alone.
Eyes cast down, words that falter!—
just as a pocket knife snaps shut,
she seized me by the hair,
and the little lad was caught.

Only God knows with which shepherd
she's carrying on again!
I must tuck up my clothes to wade in the sea,
however the wind blows and roars.
When, as often happens, I feel sorry for
the large and small fry in my net,
I would still like to be embraced
by her arms!

## *Prooemium*

In the name of Him Who created Himself,
Whose task was creation from the beginning of time!
In the name of Him Who creates faith,
trust, love, activity, and strength;
in the name of Him Who, so often named,
has always remained unknown as to His essence:

As far as the ears and eyes reach,
you find only familiar things that resemble Him,
and the loftiest fiery flight of your spirit
is already satisfied with that resemblance, with that image;
it attracts you, it carries you cheerfully away,
and wherever you roam, paths and places are adorned;
you no longer count or calculate any lapse of time,
and every step you take is immeasurability.

## Urworte. Orphisch

### ΔAIMΩN, Dämon

Wie an dem Tag, der dich der Welt verliehen,
Die Sonne stand zum Gruße der Planeten,
Bist alsobald und fort und fort gediehen
Nach dem Gesetz, wonach du angetreten.
So mußt du sein, dir kannst du nicht entfliehen,
so sagten schon Sibyllen, so Propheten;
Und keine Zeit und keine Macht zerstückelt
Geprägte Form, die lebend sich entwickelt.

### TYXH, das Zufällige

Die strenge Grenze doch umgeht gefällig
Ein Wandelndes, das mit und um uns wandelt;
Nicht einsam bleibst du, bildest dich gesellig,
Und handelst wohl so, wie ein andrer handelt:
Im Leben ists bald hin- bald widerfällig,
Es ist ein Tand und wird so durchgetandelt.
Schon hat sich still der Jahre Kreis geründet,
Die Lampe harrt der Flamme, die entzündet.

### EPΩΣ, Liebe

Die bleibt nicht aus! – Er stürzt vom Himmel nieder,
Wohin er sich aus alter Öde schwang,
Er schwebt heran auf luftigem Gefieder
Um Stirn und Brust den Frühlingstag entlang,
Scheint jetzt zu fliehn, vom Fliehen kehrt er wieder:
Da wird ein Wohl im Weh, so süß und bang.
Gar manches Herz verschwebt im Allgemeinen,
Doch widmet sich das edelste dem Einen.

### ANAΓKH, Nötigung

Da ists denn wieder, wie die Sterne wollten:
Bedingung und Gesetz, und aller Wille
Ist nur ein Wollen, weil wir eben sollten,
Und vor dem Willen schweigt die Willkür stille;
Das Liebste wird vom Herzen weggescholten,

# Primal Words. Orphic

## ΔΑΙΜΩΝ, Daimon

As on the day that lent you to the world
the sun stood to greet the planets,
you instantly thrived and continued to do so
in accordance with the law by which you made your appearance.
Thus you must be, you cannot escape yourself;
thus sibyls and prophets have already spoken;
and no passage of time nor any power can break into bits
a molded form that develops as it lives.

## ΤΥΧΗ, Chance

And yet a roving force that moves with and around us
circumvents the strict boundary as it pleases;
you do not remain alone, you are formed in society,
and most likely you act as someone else acts:
in life things fall out now this way, now that;
it is a toy and we toy our way through it.
The round of years has soon quietly come full circle:
the lamp awaits the flame that will light it.

## ΕΡΩΣ, Love

It does not fail to appear! He dives down from heaven,
up to which he rose from the ancient wasteland;
he hovers near on his airy wings
around your brow and breast throughout the spring day,
now seeming to flee, now returning from his flight;
then you feel pleasure in pain, so sweet and frightening.
Many a heart drifts away in a generalized love,
but the noblest heart devotes itself to just one.

## ΑΝΑΓΚΗ, Necessity

Then things are once again the way the stars wanted them:
stipulation and law; and all our will
consists merely in wanting things just because we ought to;
and, faced with this will, our freedom of choice falls silent:
what we love best we drive from our heart with curses,

Dem harten Muß bequemt sich Will und Grille.
So sind wir scheinfrei denn nach manchen Jahren
Nur enger dran, als wir am Anfang waren.

## ΕΛΠΙΣ, *Hoffnung*

Doch solcher Grenze, solcher ehrnen Mauer
Höchst widerwärtge Pforte wird entriegelt,
Sie stehe nur mit alter Felsendauer!
Ein Wesen regt sich leicht und ungezügelt:
Aus Wolkendecke, Nebel, Regenschauer
Erhebt sie uns, mit ihr, durch sie beflügelt,
Ihr kennt sie wohl, sie schwärmt durch alle Zonen;
Ein Flügelschlag – und hinter uns Äonen!

## *Eins und alles*

Im Grenzenlosen sich zu finden,
Wird gern der einzelne verschwinden,
Da löst sich aller Überdruß;
Statt heißem Wünschen, wildem Wollen,
Statt lästgem Fordern, strengem Sollen
Sich aufzugeben ist Genuß.

Weltseele, komm, uns zu durchdringen!
Dann mit dem Weltgeist selbst zu ringen,
Wird unsrer Kräfte Hochberuf.
Teilnehmend führen gute Geister,
Gelinde leitend höchste Meister
Zu dem, der alles schafft und schuf.

Und umzuschaffen das Geschaffne,
Damit sichs nicht zum Starren waffne,
Wirkt ewiges, lebendiges Tun.
Und was nicht war, nun will es werden
Zu reinen Sonnen, farbigen Erden;
In keinem Falle darf es ruhn.

Es soll sich regen, schaffend handeln,
Erst sich gestalten, dann verwandeln;
Nur scheinbar stehts Momente still.

both our will and our caprice submit to the hard "must."
So, then, our freedom being just an illusion, after many years
we are merely more closely confined than we were at the outset.

## ΕΛΠΙΣ, *Hope*

But the highly repugnant gateway of such limitations,
of such an unbreachable wall, is unbarred,
even if it stands with the permanence of ancient cliffs!
A being stirs lightly and unbridled:
out of the cloud cover, mist, and rain shower
it raises us, along with itself, endowing us with wings;
you surely know it, it roves through every clime;
a wing beat—and eons are behind us!

## The One and the All

To find himself in the limitless,
the individual will gladly disappear;
there all satiety is overcome;
instead of ardent wishes, violent desires,
instead of burdensome demands, strict obligations,
self-surrender is a pleasure.

World soul, come and permeate us!
For to struggle with the world spirit itself
becomes the loftiest calling of our powers.
Sympathetically, good spirits lead us;
gently, the greatest masters guide us
to the One Who creates and created everything.

And, to recreate what has been created—
so that it does not take up arms to stay the same and become rigid—
eternal, lively activity is at work.
And that which did not exist, now it will become
clear suns, colorful planets;
in no case may it be allowed to rest.

It must stir and act creatively,
first shaping itself, then transforming itself;
only seemingly does it stand still for a few moments.

Das Ewige regt sich fort in allen:
Denn alles muß in Nichts zerfallen,
Wenn es im Sein beharren will.

# Paria

## Des Paria Gebet

Großer Brahma, Herr der Mächte!
Alles ist von deinem Samen,
Und so bist du der Gerechte!
Hast du denn allein die Brahmen,
Nur die Rajahs und die Reichen,
Hast du sie allein geschaffen?
Oder bist auch du's, der Affen
Werden ließ und unseresgleichen?

Edel sind wir nicht zu nennen:
Denn das Schlechte, das gehört uns,
Und was andre tödlich kennen,
Das alleine, das vermehrt uns.
Mag dies für die Menschen gelten,
Mögen sie uns doch verachten;
Aber du, du sollst uns achten,
Denn du könntest alle schelten.

Also, Herr, nach diesem Flehen,
Segne mich zu deinem Kinde;
Oder eines laß entstehen,
Das auch mich mit dir verbinde!
Denn du hast den Bajaderen
Eine Göttin selbst erhoben;
Auch wir andern, dich zu loben,
Wollen solch ein Wunder hören.

## Legende

Wasser holen geht die reine,
Schöne Frau des hohen Brahmen,
Des verehrten, fehlerlosen,
Ernstester Gerechtigkeit.

The Eternal is constantly astir in all things:
for everything would have to crumble into nothingness
if it insisted on remaining in its momentary state.

# Pariah

## The Pariah's Prayer

Great Brahma, Lord of powers!
Everything comes from your seed,
and so you are the dispenser of justice!
Did you, then, create only the brahmans,
only the rajahs and the wealthy merchants,
them alone?
Or are you also the one who brought into being
monkeys and the likes of us?

We cannot be called noble and refined:
for it is the inferior things that belong to us;
and what others consider deadly,
that alone increases our numbers.
Let that opinion hold good for human beings,
let them despise us;
but you, you ought to respect us
because you could find fault with everybody.

And so, Lord, after this prayer,
bless me as a child of yours;
or else let something occur
that will connect even me with you!
For you have even raised up
a goddess for the bayaderes;
we others, too, so we can praise you,
wish to hear such a miracle.

## Legend

Off to fetch water goes the pure,
beautiful wife of the high priest,
that man so revered, so flawless,
of such grave righteousness.

Täglich von dem heiligen Flusse
Holt sie köstliches Erquicken –
Aber wo ist Krug und Eimer?
Sie bedarf derselben nicht.
Seligem Herzen, frommen Händen
Ballt sich die bewegte Welle
Herrlich zu kristallner Kugel;
Diese trägt sie, frohen Busens,
Reiner Sitte, holden Wandelns,
Vor den Gatten in das Haus.

Heute kommt die morgendliche
Im Gebet zu Ganges' Fluten,
Beugt sich zu der klaren Fläche –
Plötzlich überraschend spiegelt,
Aus den höchsten Himmels Breiten
Über ihr vorübereilend,
Allerlieblichste Gestalt
Hehren Jünglings, den des Gottes
Uranfänglich schönes Denken
Aus dem ewgen Busen schuf.
Solchen schauend, fühlt ergriffen
Von verwirrenden Gefühlen
Sie das innere tiefste Leben,
Will verharren in dem Anschaun,
Weist es weg, da kehrt es wieder,
Und verworren strebt sie flutwärts,
Mit unsichrer Hand zu schöpfen;
Aber ach! sie schöpft nicht mehr!
Denn des Wassers heilige Welle
Scheint zu fliehn, sich zu entfernen;
Sie erblickt nur hohler Wirbel
Grause Tiefen unter sich.

Arme sinken, Tritte straucheln,
Ists denn auch der Pfad nach Hause?
Soll sie zaudern? soll sie fliehen?
Will sie denken, wo Gedanke,
Rat und Hilfe gleich versagt? –
Und so tritt sie vor den Gatten;

Daily from the sacred river
he brings precious refreshment—
but where are her pitcher and bucket?
She has no need of such things.
For a blissful heart, for pious hands
the running water shapes itself
into a splendid crystal sphere;
this she carries, happy at heart,
pure in morals, lovely in her ways,
home to her husband.

Today she comes early in the morning
to the waves of the Ganges in prayer,
bending over the clear surface—
suddenly, taking her by surprise, there is reflected,
hastening by above her
out of the expanse of the highest heaven,
the extremely lovely form
of an exalted youth, whom the god's
beautiful mind, at the very beginning of time,
created from the bosom of the eternal.
Seeing him, she feels
her innermost, deepest life force
seized by confusing emotions;
she wishes to linger in that state of gazing;
she rejects it but it comes back again;
and in confusion she arduously returns to the river,
to draw water with an unsteady hand;
but, alas, she can no longer draw any!
For the water's sacred waves
seem to run away, to withdraw;
all she sees below her
is the horrible depths of hollow whirlpools.

Her arms sink, her steps stumble;
is this, then, her homeward path?
Should she hang back? Should she run away?
Can she think, when thoughts,
counsel, and aid all forsake her?—
And so she steps up to her husband;

Er erblickt sie, Blick ist Urteil,
Hohen Sinns ergreift das Schwert er,
Schleppt sie zu dem Totenhügel,
Wo Verbrecher büßend bluten.
Wüßte sie zu widerstreben?
Wüßte sie sich zu entschuldgen,
Schuldig, keiner Schuld bewußt?

Und er kehrt mit blutigem Schwerte
Sinnend zu der stillen Wohnung;
Da entgegnet ihm der Sohn.
»Wessen Blut ists? Vater! Vater!«–
Der Verbrecherin!–»Mitnichten!
Denn es starret nicht am Schwerte
Wie verbrecherische Tropfen,
Fließt wie aus der Wunde frisch.
Mutter, Mutter! tritt heraus her!
Ungerecht war nie der Vater,
Sage, was er jetzt verübt.«–
Schweige! Schweige! 's ist das ihre!–
»Wessen ist es?«–Schweige! Schweige!
»Wäre meiner Mutter Blut!!!
Was geschehen? was verschuldet?
Her das Schwert! ergriffen hab ichs;
Deine Gattin magst du töten,
Aber meine Mutter nicht!
In die Flammen folgt die Gattin
Ihrem einzig Angetrauten,
Seiner einzig teuren Mutter
In das Schwert der treue Sohn.«

Halt, o halte! rief der Vater,
Noch ist Raum, enteil, enteile!
Füge Haupt dem Rumpfe wieder,
Du berührest mit dem Schwerte,
Und lebendig folgt sie dir.

Eilend, atemlos erblickt er
Staunend zweier Frauen Körper
Überkreuzt, und so die Häupter–
Welch Entsetzen! welche Wahl!

ιe takes one look at her, and in that look he passes judgment;
vith a noble purpose he seizes his sword
ınd drags her to the mound of death,
vhere criminals shed their blood in penance.
Could she possibly resist?
Could she possibly excuse herself,
ζuilty but not conscious of any guilt?

And with his bloody sword he returns,
deep in thought, to his silent dwelling;
there his son meets him.
"Whose blood is this? Father! Father!"
"A female lawbreaker's!" "Not at all!
For it isn't forming solid drops on the sword
like the blood of a criminal,
but it's flowing as if fresh from the wound.
Mother, Mother, come out here!
Father has never been unjust,
tell me what injustice he has committed now!"
"Quiet, quiet! It's hers."
"It's whose?" "Quiet, quiet!"
"Could it be my mother's blood?
What happened? What wrong did she commit?
Give me the sword! Now I've got it!
You may kill your wife,
but not my mother!
Into the flames a wife follows
the one and only man she has married;
the loyal son follows onto the sword
his one and only dear mother."

"Stop, stop!" cried his father,
"There's still time, hurry, hurry!
Join her head to her body again;
just touch her with the sword
and she'll follow you, a living woman."

In haste, out of breath, he sees
to his amazement the bodies of two women,
one lying across the other, and the heads also—
what horror! What a choice to make!

Dann der Mutter Haupt erfaßt er,
Küßt es nicht, das tot erblaßte;
Auf des nächsten Rumpfes Lücke
Setzt ers eilig, mit dem Schwerte
Segnet er das fromme Werk.

Aufersteht ein Riesenbildnis. –
Von der Mutter teuren Lippen,
Göttlich-unverändert-süßen,
Tönt das grausenvolle Wort:
Sohn, o Sohn! welch Übereilen!
Deiner Mutter Leichnam dorten,
Neben ihm das freche Haupt
Der Verbrecherin, des Opfers
Waltender Gerechtigkeit!
Mich nun hast du ihrem Körper
Eingeimpft auf ewige Tage:
Weisen Wollens, wilden Handelns
Werd ich unter Göttern sein;
Ja, des Himmelsknaben Bildnis
Webt so schön vor Stirn und Auge –
Senkt sichs in das Herz herunter,
Regt es tolle Wutbegier.
Immer wird es wiederkehren,
Immer steigen, immer sinken,
Sich verdüstern, sich verklären,
So hat Brahma dies gewollt.
Er gebot ja buntem Fittich,
Klarem Antlitz, schlanken Gliedern,
Göttlich-einzigem Erscheinen
Mich zu prüfen, zu verführen;
Denn von oben kommt Verführung,
Wenns den Göttern so beliebt.
Und so soll ich, die Brahmane,
Mit dem Haupt im Himmel weilend,
Fühlen, Paria, dieser Erde
Niederziehende Gewalt.

Sohn, ich sende dich dem Vater!
Tröste! – Nicht ein traurig Büßen,
Stumpfes Harren, stolz Verdienen

Then he seizes his mother's head,
pale in death, but doesn't kiss it;
he hastily places it in the empty place
on the nearest body; with the sword
he blesses his pious act.

There arises from death a gigantic form.—
From his mother's dear lips,
divinely sweet and unchanged,
come the terrifying words:
'Son, my son, what reckless haste!
That is your mother's corpse there,
next to it the insolent head
of the criminal, the victim
of prevailing justice!
You have now grafted me
onto her body forever:
among the gods I shall be
wise in my thinking, wild in my actions;
yes, the image of that heaven-dwelling boy
hovers so beautifully before my brow and my eyes—
it descends to my heart,
stirring up insane, raging desire.
It will always come back again,
always rising, always sinking,
growing dim and growing bright;
thus has Brahma decreed.
For he commanded those colorful wings,
that bright face, those slender limbs,
that unique godlike vision,
to test me, to seduce me;
for seduction comes from up above
when it so pleases the gods.
And so I, the brahman woman,
tarrying in heaven with my head,
shall feel, as a pariah, the power
of this earth, which drags one down.

"Son, I send you to your father!
Console him!—Let not sorrowful penance,
stolid lingering, or pride in meritorious actions,

Halt euch in der Wildnis fest;
Wandert aus durch alle Welten,
Wandelt hin durch alle Zeiten
Und verkündet auch Geringstem:
Daß ihn Brahma droben hört!

Ihm ist keiner der Geringste –
Wer sich mit gelähmten Gliedern,
Sich mit wild zerstörtem Geiste,
Düster, ohne Hilf und Rettung,
Sei er Brahma, sei er Paria,
Mit dem Blick nach oben kehrt,
Wirds empfinden, wirds erfahren:
Dort erglühen tausend Augen,
Ruhend lauschen tausend Ohren,
Denen nichts verborgen bleibt.

Heb ich mich zu seinem Throne,
Schaut er mich, die Grausenhafte,
Die er gräßlich umgeschaffen,
Muß er ewig mich bejammern,
Euch zugute komme das.
Und ich werd ihn freundlich mahnen,
Und ich werd ihm wütend sagen,
Wie es mir der Sinn gebietet,
Wie es mir im Busen schwellet.
Was ich denke, was ich fühle –
Ein Geheimnis bleibe das.

## Dank des Paria

Großer Brahma! nun erkenn ich,
Daß du Schöpfer bist der Welten!
Dich als meinen Herrscher nenn ich,
Denn du lässest alle gelten.

Und verschließest auch dem Letzten
Keines von den tausend Ohren;
Uns, die tief Herabgesetzten,
Alle hast du neu geboren.

keep the two of you in the wilderness;
wander out all over the world,
keep wandering all through time
and proclaim it even to the lowliest:
that Brahma up above hears him!

"For him no man is the lowliest—
whoever, with paralyzed limbs,
with a wildly deranged mind,
gloomy, without aid or salvation,
be he a brahman, be he a pariah,
turns his eyes upward
will feel this, will experience it:
there a thousand eyes gleam,
a thousand ears listen in repose,
from which nothing remains concealed.

"If I raise myself to his throne,
if he looks at me, horrible as I am,
me whom he transformed in a grisly manner,
if he must eternally pity me,
let that turn out to your advantage.
And I shall amiably remind him,
and I shall speak to him in rage,
just as my mind commands me to,
just as my heart pounds in my breast.
What I think, what I feel—
let that remain a mystery."

## The Pariah's Thanks

Great Brahma, now I realize
that you are the creator of the worlds!
I call you my sovereign
because you find value in everyone.

And even for the humblest you shut
not one of your thousand ears;
to all of us, the deeply disparaged,
you have given birth anew.

Wendet euch zu dieser Frauen,
Die der Schmerz zur Göttin wandelt!
Nun beharr ich, anzuschauen
Den, der einzig wirkt und handelt.

## An Madame Marie Szymanowska [Aussöhnung]

Die Leidenschaft bringt Leiden! – Wer beschwichtigt,
Beklommnes Herz, dich, das zu viel verloren?
Wo sind die Stunden, überschnell verflüchtigt?
Vergebens war das Schönste dir erkoren!
Trüb ist der Geist, verworren das Beginnen;
Die hehre Welt, wie schwindet sie den Sinnen!

Da schwebt hervor Musik mit Engelsschwingen,
Verflicht zu Millionen Tön um Töne,
Des Menschen Wesen durch und durch zu dringen,
Zu überfüllen ihn mit ewger Schöne:
Das Auge netzt sich, fühlt im höhern Sehnen
Den Götter-Wert der Töne wie der Tränen.

Und so das Herz erleichtert merkt behende,
Daß es noch lebt und schlägt und möchte schlagen,
Zum reinsten Dank der überreichen Spende
Sich selbst erwidernd willig darzutragen.
Da fühlte sich – o daß es ewig bliebe! –
Das Doppel-Glück der Töne wie der Liebe.

## Elegie

Und wenn der Mensch in seiner Qual verstummt,
Gab mir ein Gott, zu sagen, was ich leide.

Was soll ich nun vom Wiedersehen hoffen,
von dieses Tages noch geschloßner Blüte?
Das Paradies, die Hölle steht dir offen;
Wie wankelsinnig regt sichs im Gemüte! –
Kein Zweifeln mehr! Sie tritt ans Himmelstor,
Zu ihren Armen hebt sie dich empor.

People, turn your eyes toward that woman,
whom sorrow transforms into a goddess!
Now I dwell in contemplation
of him, the only one who exerts power and performs actions.

## To Madame Marie Szymanowska [Reconciliation]

Passion brings suffering!—Uneasy heart,
who can soothe you, you that have lost too much?
Where are the hours, vanished too quickly?
The most beautiful thing was chosen for you in vain!
Sad is our mind, confused are our endeavors;
how the lofty world fades away from our senses!

And then music hovers by on its angel's wings,
interweaving one tone with another into millions,
in order to penetrate man's being through and through,
to fill him overabundantly with eternal beauty:
his eyes grow moist, in a higher yearning
they feel the divine worth of music and of tears.

And so the relieved heart quickly notices
that it still lives and beats and wishes to go on beating,
so it can offer itself willingly in return,
in sincerest thanks for that more than generous gift.
Then came the sensation—may it remain forever!—
of the double happiness of music and of love.

## Elegy

And when mortals fall silent in their torment,
a god granted me the power of expressing my suffering.

What am I now to hope for from this meeting,
from this day's blossom, still enclosed in its bud?
Both paradise and hell are open to you;
what changeable stirrings in my mind!—
No more doubts! She arrives at heaven's gate,
and raises you up to her arms.

So warst du denn im Paradies empfangen,
Als wärst du wert des ewig schönen Lebens;
Dir blieb kein Wunsch, kein Hoffen, kein Verlangen,
Hier war das Ziel des innigsten Bestrebens,
Und in dem Anschaun dieses einzig Schönen
Versiegte gleich der Quell sehnsüchtiger Tränen.

Wie regte nicht der Tag die raschen Flügel,
Schien die Minuten vor sich her zu treiben!
Der Abendkuß, ein treu verbindlich Siegel:
So wird es auch der nächsten Sonne bleiben.
Die Stunden glichen sich in zartem Wandern
Wie Schwestern zwar, doch keine ganz den andern.

Der Kuß, der letzte, grausam süß, zerschneidend
Ein herrliches Geflecht verschlungner Minnen.
Nun eilt, nun stockt der Fuß, die Schwelle meidend,
Als trieb' ein Cherub flammend ihn von hinnen;
Das Auge starrt auf düstrem Pfad verdrossen,
Es blickt zurück, die Pforte steht verschlossen.

Und nun verschlossen in sich selbst, als hätte
Dies Herz sich nie geöffnet, selige Stunden
Mit jedem Stern des Himmels um die Wette
An ihrer Seite leuchtend nicht empfunden;
Und Mißmut, Reue, Vorwurf, Sorgenschwere
Belastens nun in schwüler Atmosphäre.

Ist denn die Welt nicht übrig? Felsenwände,
Sind sie nicht mehr gekrönt von heiligen Schatten?
Die Ernte, reift sie nicht? Ein grün Gelände,
Zieht sichs nicht hin am Fluß durch Busch und Matten?
Und wölbt sich nicht das überweltlich Große,
Gestaltenreiche, bald Gestaltenlose?

Wie leicht und zierlich, klar und zart gewoben
Schwebt, seraphgleich, aus ernster Wolken Chor,
Als glich' es ihr, am blauen Äther droben
Ein schlank Gebild aus lichtem Duft empor!
So sahst du sie in frohem Tanze walten,
Die lieblichste der lieblichsten Gestalten.

And so you were received in paradise
as if you were worthy of an eternal, beautiful life;
your every wish, hope, desire was fulfilled;
here was the goal of your most ardent striving;
and at the sight of that unique beauty
the fountain of yearning tears at once dried up.

How the day beat its swift wings,
seeming to chase the minutes before it!
The kiss at evening, a seal pledging fidelity:
and so it will remain on the following day.
In their soft passage the hours resembled one another
like sisters, yes, but none exactly like the others.

That final kiss, cruelly sweet, slicing through
a splendid fabric of intertwined amorous relations.
My feet now hasten, now falter, avoiding the threshold,
as if a flaming cherub were driving them away;
my eyes stare in vexation on my dark path;
they look back, the portal is locked.

And now my heart is locked inside itself, as if
it had never opened, as if it had never enjoyed
blissful hours, glowing, at her side,
in rivalry with every star in the sky;
and moroseness, regret, reproach, and heavy cares
now weigh it down in a sultry atmosphere.

Doesn't the world remain to me? Cliff walls,
are they no longer crowned by holy shadows?
Doesn't the harvest still ripen? Doesn't a green countryside
extend along the river with bushes and meadows?
And doesn't the greatness of a higher world arch over me,
now full of forms, now devoid of forms?

How lightly and charmingly, woven clearly and tenderly,
like a seraph, a slender image of bright mist
hovers upward from a chorus of solemn clouds
in the blue sky above, as if it resembled her!
That's how you saw her presiding over the merry dance,
the loveliest of loveliest forms.

Doch nur Momente darfst dich unterwinden,
Ein Luftgebild statt ihrer festzuhalten;
Ins Herz zurück! dort wirst du's besser finden,
Dort regt sie sich in wechselnden Gestalten:
Zu Vielen bildet Eine sich hinüber,
So tausendfach, und immer, immer lieber.

Wie zum Empfang sie an den Pforten weilte
Und mich von dannauf stufenweis beglückte,
Selbst nach dem letzten Kuß mich noch ereilte,
Den letztesten mir auf die Lippen drückte:
So klar beweglich bleibt das Bild der Lieben,
Mit Flammenschrift, ins treue Herz geschrieben.

Ins Herz, das fest, wie zinnenhohe Mauer,
Sich ihr bewahrt und sie in sich bewahret,
Für sie sich freut an seiner eignen Dauer,
Nur weiß von sich, wenn sie sich offenbaret,
Sich freier fühlt in so geliebten Schranken
Und nur noch schlägt, für alles ihr zu danken.

War Fähigkeit, zu lieben, war Bedürfen
Von Gegenliebe weggelöscht, verschwunden,
Ist Hoffnungslust zu freudigen Entwürfen,
Entschlüssen, rascher Tat sogleich gefunden!
Wenn Liebe je den Liebenden begeistet,
Ward es an mir aufs lieblichste geleistet;

Und zwar durch sie! – Wie lag ein innres Bangen
Auf Geist und Körper, unwillkommner Schwere:
Von Schauerbildern rings der Blick umfangen
Im wüsten Raum beklommner Herzensleere;
Nun dämmert Hoffnung von bekannter Schwelle,
Sie selbst erscheint in milder Sonnenhelle.

Dem Frieden Gottes, welcher euch hienieden
Mehr als Vernunft beseliget – wir lesens –
Vergleich ich wohl der Liebe heitern Frieden
In Gegenwart des allgeliebten Wesens;
Da ruht das Herz, und nichts vermag zu stören
Den tiefsten Sinn, den Sinn: ihr zu gehören.

But only for moments are you allowed to endeavor
to hold onto an airy image instead of her;
back into my heart! There you'll be better off,
where she moves about in changing forms:
a single form is transmuted into multiple ones,
a thousandfold, and dearer with each moment.

Just as she lingered by the gate to await me
and made me happy as we ascended step by step,
still catching up with me even after the last kiss
and pressing the very, very last upon my lips:
so the picture of my sweetheart remains clear and mobile,
drawn on my faithful heart with lines of flame—

on my heart, which as firm as a high, battlemented wall,
preserves itself for her and her within itself,
which rejoices in its own continuance for her sake,
which is aware of itself only when she manifests herself,
which feels more free within such beloved confines,
and only keeps on beating in order to thank her for everything.

If my capacity to love, if my need
for requited love were previously wiped out and gone,
the hopeful desire for happy plans,
decisions, and quick action was rediscovered immediately!
If love ever fills the lover with enthusiasm,
that service was done for me in the loveliest way—

of course, through her! What a great inner fear
oppressed my mind and body with an unwelcome burden:
my eyes were surrounded by images of terror
in the chaotic void of an uneasy heart;
now hope dawns from a familiar threshold,
she herself appears in gentle sunlight.

I may compare the serene peace of love
in the presence of the all-beloved being
to that peace of God which here on earth
makes us happier than our reason does, as we read;
then the heart rests, and nothing can disturb
the profound thought, the thought that it belongs to her.

In unsers Busens Reine wogt ein Streben,
Sich einem Höhern, Reinern, Unbekannten
Aus Dankbarkeit freiwillig hinzugeben,
Enträtselnd sich den ewig Ungenannten;
Wir heißens: fromm sein! – Solcher seligen Höhe
Fühl ich mich teilhaft, wenn ich vor ihr stehe.

Vor ihrem Blick, wie vor der Sonne Walten,
Vor ihrem Atem, wie vor Frühlingslüften,
Zerschmilzt, so längst sich eisig starr gehalten,
Der Selbstsinn tief in winterlichen Grüften;
Kein Eigennutz, kein Eigenwille dauert,
Vor ihrem Kommen sind sie weggeschauert.

Es ist, als wenn sie sagte: »Stund um Stunde
Wird uns das Leben freundlich dargeboten.
Das Gestrige ließ uns geringe Kunde,
Das Morgende – zu wissen ists verboten;
Und wenn ich je mich vor dem Abend scheute,
Die Sonne sank und sah noch, was mich freute.

Drum tu wie ich und schaue, froh verständig,
Dem Augenblick ins Auge! Kein Verschieben!
Begegn ihm schnell, wohlwollend wie lebendig,
Im Handeln, sei's zu Freude sei's dem Lieben.
Nur wo du bist, sei alles, immer kindlich,
So bist du alles, bist unüberwindlich.«

Du hast gut reden, dacht ich: zum Geleite
Gab dir ein Gott die Gunst des Augenblickes,
Und jeder fühlt an deiner holden Seite
Sich augenblicks den Günstling des Geschickes;
Mich schreckt der Wink, von dir mich zu entfernen –
Was hilft es mir, so hohe Weisheit lernen!

Nun bin ich fern! Der jetzigen Minute,
Was ziemt denn der? Ich wüßt es nicht zu sagen;
Sie bietet mir zum Schönen manches Gute,
Das lastet nur, ich muß mich ihm entschlagen.
Mich treibt umher ein unbezwinglich Sehnen,
Da bleibt kein Rat als grenzenlose Tränen.

nto the purity of our breast surges the ambition
o dedicate ourselves, voluntarily, out of gratitude,
o something higher, purer, unknown,
solving the puzzle of the eternally Unnamed;
ve call this "being pious"!—I feel as if I have a share
n such blissful heights when I stand before her.

Before her eyes, as in the strength of the sun;
before her breath, as before spring breezes,
he egotism that has long remained icily rigid,
deep in wintry graves, melts away;
no selfishness, no stubbornness lasts;
they are scoured away at her approach.

It is as if she said: "Hour after hour
life is amiably offered to us.
Yesterday left us with little information,
tomorrow—it is forbidden to know;
and if I ever feared the coming of evening,
the setting sun still looked down on things that rejoiced me.

"And so, do as I do, and, with a cheerful understanding,
look each moment in the eye! No procrastination!
Meet it quickly, benevolently, and briskly
in your actions, in your joy, and in your loving.
Wherever you are, be all these things, always childlike,
and so you will be everything, you will be unconquerable."

"It's easy for you to say that," thought I; "as an escort
some god gave you each moment's good graces,
and by your dear side everyone feels
he is momentarily the favorite of fate;
I fear the signal for departing from you—
What good does it do me to learn such lofty wisdom?"

Now I am far from you! What is fitting
for the present minute? I couldn't say;
it offers me many good things along with the beautiful,
but that is only a burden; I must get rid of it.
I'm driven about by an unsubduable yearning,
the only recourse I have left is unending tears.

So quellt denn fort! und fließet unaufhaltsam;
Doch nie gelängs, die innre Glut zu dämpfen!
Schon rasts und reißt in meiner Brust gewaltsam,
Wo Tod und Leben grausend sich bekämpfen.
Wohl Kräuter gäbs, des Körpers Qual zu stillen;
Allein dem Geist fehlts am Entschluß und Willen,

Fehlts am Begriff: wie sollt er sie vermissen?
Er wiederholt ihr Bild zu tausendmalen.
Das zaudert bald, bald wird es weggerissen,
Undeutlich jetzt und jetzt im reinsten Strahlen;
Wie könnte dies geringstem Troste frommen,
Die Ebb und Flut, das Gehen wie das Kommen?

∗

Verlaßt mich hier, getreue Weggenossen!
Laßt mich allein am Fels, in Moor und Moos;
Nur immer zu! euch ist die Welt erschlossen,
Die Erde weit, der Himmel hehr und groß;
Betrachtet, forscht, die Einzelheiten sammelt,
Naturgeheimnis werde nachgestammelt.

Mir ist das All, ich bin mir selbst verloren,
Der ich noch erst den Göttern Liebling war;
Sie prüften mich, verliehen mir Pandoren,
So reich an Gütern, reicher an Gefahr;
Sie drängten mich zum gabeseligen Munde,
Sie trennen mich, und richten mich zugrunde.

## An Werther

Noch einmal wagst du, vielbeweinter Schatten,
Hervor dich an das Tageslicht,
Begegnest mir auf neu beblümten Matten,
Und meinen Anblick scheust du nicht.
Es ist, als ob du lebtest in der Frühe,
Wo uns der Tau auf Einem Feld erquickt
Und nach des Tages unwillkommner Mühe

So gush forth and flow uncontrollably;
but may you never succeed in quenching my inner flame!
There is already powerful raving and laceration in my breast,
where death and life are waging a horrible battle.
There may be herbs to soothe my body's torment;
but my mind lacks decision and will power,

it lacks the very notion: how can it do without her?
It repeats her image thousands of times.
Now the picture lingers, now it is torn away,
now it is indistinct and now lit by the brightest beams;
how can this help with even the slightest consolation,
this ebb and flow, this going and coming?

\*

Leave me here, my loyal travel companions!
Leave me alone on crag, heath, and moor;
keep on going! For you the world lies open,
the earth is broad, the sky lofty and great;
contemplate, do research, gather details,
let the secrets of nature be probed, if only haltingly.

I have lost the universe, I am even lost to myself,
I who recently was still the favorite of the gods;
they tested me, they lent me Pandora,
so rich in possessions, richer in danger;
they thrust me toward those gift-bestowing lips;
now they separate me from them and utterly destroy me.

## To Werther

Once again, much-lamented shade, you venture
out into the light of day,
you meet me on meadows filled with new flowers,
and you do not avoid the sight of me.
It is as if you lived in the morning hours,
when we are refreshed by the dew on one field
and, after the unwelcome labors of the day,

Der Scheidesonne letzter Strahl entzückt;
Zum Bleiben ich, zum Scheiden du erkoren,
Gingst du voran – und hast nicht viel verloren.

Des Menschen Leben scheint ein herrlich Los:
Der Tag wie lieblich, so die Nacht wie groß!
Und wir, gepflanzt in Paradieses Wonne,
Genießen kaum der hocherlauchten Sonne,
Da kämpft sogleich verworrene Bestrebung
Bald mit uns selbst und bald mit der Umgebung;
Keins wird vom andern wünschenswert ergänzt,
Von außen düsterts, wenn es innen glänzt,
Ein glänzend Äußres deckt ein trüber Blick,
Da steht es nah – und man verkennt das Glück.

Nun glauben wirs zu kennen! Mit Gewalt
Ergreift uns Liebreiz weiblicher Gestalt:
Der Jüngling, froh wie in der Kindheit Flor,
Im Frühling tritt als Frühling selbst hervor,
Entzückt, erstaunt, wer dies ihm angetan?
Er schaut umher, die Welt gehört ihm an.
Ins Weite zieht ihn unbefangne Hast,
Nichts engt ihn ein, nicht Mauer, nicht Palast;
Wie Vögelschar an Wäldergipfeln streift,
So schwebt auch er, der um die Liebste schweift,
Er sucht vom Äther, den er gern verläßt,
Den treuen Blick, und dieser hält ihn fest.

Doch erst zu früh und dann zu spät gewarnt,
Fühlt er den Flug gehemmt, fühlt sich umgarnt.
Das Wiedersehn ist froh, das Scheiden schwer,
Das Wieder-Wiedersehn beglückt noch mehr,
Und Jahre sind im Augenblick ersetzt;
Doch tückisch harrt das Lebewohl zuletzt.

Du lächelst, Freund, gefühlvoll, wie sich ziemt:
Ein gräßlich Scheiden machte dich berühmt;
Wir feierten dein kläglich Mißgeschick,
Du ließest uns zu Wohl und Weh zurück.
Dann zog uns wieder ungewisse Bahn
Der Leidenschaften labyrinthisch an;

are delighted by the last rays of the departing sun;
I was chosen as one to remain; you, as one chosen to depart,
left before me—and didn't lose much.

Human life seems like a splendid winning lot:
how lovely the day, how great the night!
And we, planted in the rapture of paradise,
hardly get to enjoy the sun shining high above
when, at once, a confused ambition
fights now against us, now against our environment;
no one thing is complemented by another in a desirable way;
there is gloom outside us whenever there is brightness within;
a bright exterior is concealed by a dismal glance;
it's right near us—and we fail to recognize our happiness.

Now we think we recognize it! With force
the charms of a woman's form seize us:
the young man, as happy as when in the bloom of childhood,
steps forth in springtime, himself like the spring,
delighted, wondering who has bewitched him so.
He looks around, the world is his.
Ingenuous haste draws him to far-off places;
nothing closes him in, neither walls nor palaces;
as a flock of birds darts past forested peaks,
so he, too, soars, roaming around his sweetheart;
from the heavens, which he gladly abandons,
he seeks the faithful eyes, which hold him fast.

But warned, first too early and then too late,
he feels his flight impeded, he feels himself ensnared.
A second meeting is happy, the parting is difficult,
a further meeting makes him even happier,
and years are compensated for in the passing moment;
still, a good-bye is finally, spitefully, in store for him.

You smile, my friend, sentimentally, as is befitting:
a horrible departure made you famous;
we mourned your lamentable misfortune,
you left us behind for weal or woe.
Then the uncertain path of passions
drew us again into its labyrinth;

Und wir, verschlungen wiederholter Not,
Dem Scheiden endlich – Scheiden ist der Tod!
Wie klingt es rührend, wenn der Dichter singt,
Den Tod zu meiden, den das Scheiden bringt!
Verstrickt in solche Qualen, halbverschuldet,
Geb ihm ein Gott, zu sagen, was er duldet.

## Bei Betrachtung von Schillers Schädel

Im ernsten Beinhaus wars, wo ich beschaute,
   Wie Schädel Schädeln angeordnet paßten;
   Die alte Zeit gedacht ich, die ergraute.
Sie stehn in Reih geklemmt, die sonst sich haßten,
   Und derbe Knochen, die sich tödlich schlugen,
   Sie liegen kreuzweis, zahm allhier zu rasten.
Entrenkte Schulterblätter! was sie trugen,
   Fragt niemand mehr, und zierlich tätge Glieder,
   Die Hand, der Fuß, zerstreut aus Lebensfugen.
Ihr Müden also lagt vergebens nieder,
   Nicht Ruh im Grabe ließ man euch, vertrieben
   Seid ihr herauf zum lichten Tage wieder,
Und niemand kann die dürre Schale lieben,
   Welch herrlich edlen Kern sie auch bewahrte.
   Doch mir Adepten war die Schrift geschrieben,
Die heilgen Sinn nicht jedem offenbarte,
   Als ich inmitten solcher starren Menge
   Unschätzbar herrlich ein Gebild gewahrte,
Daß in des Raumes Moderkält und Enge
   Ich frei und wärmefühlend mich erquickte,
   Als ob ein Lebensquell dem Tod entspränge.
Wie mich geheimnisvoll die Form entzückte!
   Die gottgedachte Spur, die sich erhalten!
   Ein Blick, der mich an jenes Meer entrückte,
Das flutend strömt gesteigerte Gestalten.
   Geheim Gefäß! Orakelsprüche spendend,
   Wie bin ich wert, dich in der Hand zu halten?
Dich höchsten Schatz aus Moder fromm entwendend
   Und in die freie Luft, zu freiem Sinnen,
   Zum Sonnenlicht andächtig hin mich wendend.

nd we have been embroiled in repeated amorous plights,
inally in separation—separation is death!
Iow touching it sounds when the poet sings
n order to avoid the death that separation brings!
Intangled in such torments, half to blame,
nay a god give him the power to express what he endures.

## On Contemplating Schiller's Skull

It was in the solemn charnel house, where I observed
   how skull after skull was arranged in rows;
    I thought about past times, which have grown gray.
They stand jammed into rows, those who once hated each other,
   and rough bones, which beat each other to death,
    lie crosswise, resting here tamely.
Dislocated shoulder blades—what they carried
   no one asks any longer—and fragile, active limbs,
    hands and feet, wrenched from their normal joints and scattered around.
And so you weary ones lay down in vain;
   you weren't allowed to rest in the grave; driven out,
    you have come back up to the light of day,
and no one is able to love the dried-out shell,
   no matter how splendid and noble the kernel it once protected.
    But for me, the initiate, a message was inscribed there
which has not revealed its sacred meaning to all men,
   when in the midst of such a rigid multitude I
    espied a form incalculably splendid,
so that in the narrow room's mustiness and cold
   I felt refreshed, in a warm, wide-open space,
    as if a fountain of life was gushing out of death.
How that form delighted me mysteriously!
   The traces of divine purpose that were preserved there!—
    a sight that spirited me off to that sea
which carries enhanced forms in its rushing current.
   Mysterious container proclaiming oracles,
    how am I worthy to hold you in my hands?
Purloining you, you greatest treasure, piously from that decay,
   I turned to the open air, to open thoughts,
    to the sunlight, devoutly.

Was kann der Mensch im Leben mehr gewinnen,
    Als daß sich Gott-Natur ihm offenbare?
    Wie sie das Feste läßt zu Geist verrinnen,
    Wie sie das Geisterzeugte fest bewahre.

## "Aus den Gruben, hier im Graben"

Aus den Gruben, hier im Graben
Hör ich des Propheten Sang;
Engel schweben, ihn zu laben,
Wäre da dem Guten bang?
Löw und Löwin, hin und wieder,
Schmiegen sich um ihn heran;
Ja, die sanften, frommen Lieder
Habens ihnen angetan.

Engel schweben auf und nieder
Uns in Tönen zu erlaben,
Welch ein himmlischer Gesang!
In den Gruben, in dem Graben
Wäre da dem Kinde bang?
Diese sanften, frommen Lieder
Lassen Unglück nicht heran:
Engel schweben hin und wieder,
Und so ist es schon getan.

Denn der Ewge herrscht auf Erden,
Über Meere herrscht sein Blick;
Löwen sollen Lämmer werden,
Und die Welle schwankt zurück;
Blankes Schwert erstarrt im Hiebe,
Glaub und Hoffnung sind erfüllt;
Wundertätig ist die Liebe,
Die sich im Gebet enthüllt.

Und so geht mit guten Kindern
Selger Engel gern zu Rat,
Böses Wollen zu verhindern,
Zu befördern schöne Tat.

What more can a man win in life
　　than to have God and nature manifest themselves to him?—
　　to see how they make solid things melt into spirit,
　　how they solidly preserve that which the spirit has engendered.

## *"From out of the pit, here in the lions' den"*

From out of the pit, here in the lions' den,
　hear the prophet's song;
angels hover around to bring him refreshment;
could the good man be afraid in such a case?
Lion and lioness, back and forth,
snuggle up to him;
yes, his gentle, pious songs
have cast a spell over them.

Angels soar up and down
to refresh us with music;
what a heavenly chant!
In the pit, in the den,
could the child be afraid?
These gentle, pious songs
allow no misfortune to approach:
angels soar up and down,
and so it's already done.

For the Eternal rules on earth,
his gaze rules over the seas;
lions are to become lambs,
and the waves recede;
the drawn sword halts in mid-thrust,
faith and hope are justified;
miracle-working is that love
which reveals itself in prayer.

And so a blessed angel
gladly advises good children,
to prevent evil wishes,
to promote beautiful deeds.

So beschwören, fest zu bannen
Liebem Sohn ans zarte Knie
Ihn, des Waldes Hochtyrannen,
Frommer Sinn und Melodie.

## "Dämmrung senkte sich von oben"

Dämmrung senkte sich von oben,
Schon ist alle Nähe fern;
Doch zuerst emporgehoben
Holden Lichts der Abendstern!
Alles schwankt ins Ungewisse,
Nebel schleichen in die Höh;
Schwarzvertiefte Finsternisse
Widerspiegelnd ruht der See.

Nun im östlichen Bereiche
Ahn ich Mondenglanz und Glut,
Schlanker Weiden Haargezweige
Scherzen auf der nächsten Flut.
Durch bewegter Schatten Spiele
Zittert Lunas Zauberschein,
Und durchs Auge schleicht die Kühle
Sänftigend ins Herz hinein.

## Den Vereinigten Staaten

Amerika, du hast es besser
Als unser Kontinent, das alte,
Hast keine verfallene Schlösser
Und keine Basalte.
Dich stört nicht im Innern,
Zu lebendiger Zeit,
Unnützes Erinnern
Und vergeblicher Streit.

And so pious thoughts and melody
work their spell to hold him fast,
the arch-tyrant of the jungle,
at the tender knees of a beloved child.

## "Twilight has descended from above"

Twilight has descended from above,
now everything near is far;
but first these has arisen
the evening star with its lovely light!
Everything reels into uncertainty,
mists creep upward;
reflecting the dark, with its patches of deeper blackness,
the lake is calm.

Now in the eastern quarter
I sense the moon's light and heat;
the hairlike branches of slender willows
sport upon the nearest waves.
Through the interplay of restless shadows
Luna's magical glow trembles,
and by way of the eyes coolness creeps
soothingly into the heart.

## To the United States

America, you're better off
than our old continent;
you have no ruined castles
and no basalt.
You are not disturbed in your interior,
in this vital period,
by unprofitable memories
and vain quarrels.

Benutzt die Gegenwart mit Glück!
Und wenn nun eure Kinder dichten,
Bewahre sie ein gut Geschick
Vor Ritter-, Räuber- und Gespenstergeschichten.

## Der Bräutigam

Um Mitternacht, ich schlief, im Busen wachte
Das liebevolle Herz, als wär es Tag;
Der Tag erschien, mir war, als ob es nachte –
Was ist es mir, so viel er bringen mag?

Sie fehlte ja! mein emsig Tun und Streben
Für sie allein ertrug ichs durch die Glut
Der heißen Stunde; welch erquicktes Leben
Am kühlen Abend! lohnend wars und gut.

Die Sonne sank, und Hand in Hand verpflichtet
Begrüßten wir den letzten Segensblick,
Und Auge sprach, ins Auge klar gerichtet:
Von Osten, hoffe nur, sie kommt zurück.

Um Mitternacht, der Sterne Glanz geleitet
Im holden Traum zur Schwelle, wo sie ruht.
O sei auch mir dort auszuruhn bereitet!
Wie es auch sei, das Leben, es ist gut.

## Dem aufgehenden Vollmonde

Willst du mich sogleich verlassen?
Warst im Augenblick so nah!
Dich umfinstern Wolkenmassen,
Und nun bist du gar nicht da.

Doch du fühlst, wie ich betrübt bin,
Blickt dein Rand herauf als Stern!
Zeugest mir, daß ich geliebt bin,
Sei das Liebchen noch so fern.

Use the present day with happiness!
And when your children write,
may a kind fate preserve them
from tales of knights, highwaymen, and ghosts.

## The Bridegroom

At midnight, as I slept, my loving heart
was awake in my breast, as if it were day;
day appeared, and I felt as if it were night—
what is it to me, no matter how much the day brings?

Yes, she was missing! I had endured my busy doing
and striving through the heat of the torrid hours
for her alone; how refreshed my life was
in the cool of the evening! It was rewarding and good.

The sun set, and, hand in hand, in mutual obligation
we greeted its final rays as they bestowed blessing,
and, looking each other directly in the eye, we said:
"Just keep hoping, and it will rise again in the east."

At midnight, the light of the stars leads me
in a lovely dream to the threshold where she reposes.
Oh, may it be granted me to enjoy rest there, too!
However life may be, it is good.

## To the Rising Full Moon

Do you wish to desert me at once?
A moment ago you were so close!
You are darkened by masses of cloud,
and now you are gone altogether.

But you feel how gloomy I am;
your rim looks upward like a star!
You bear witness to me that I am loved,
no matter how far away my sweetheart is.

So hinan denn! hell und heller,
Reiner Bahn, in voller Pracht!
Schlägt mein Herz auch schmerzlich schneller,
Überselig ist die Nacht.

## Vermächtnis

Kein Wesen kann zu nichts zerfallen!
Das Ewge regt sich fort in allen,
Am Sein erhalte dich beglückt!
Das Sein ist ewig: denn Gesetze
Bewahren die lebendgen Schätze,
Aus welchen sich das All geschmückt.

Das Wahre war schon längst gefunden,
Hat edle Geisterschaft verbunden;
Das alte Wahre, faß es an!
Verdank es, Erdensohn, dem Weisen,
Der ihr, die Sonne zu umkreisen,
Und dem Geschwister wies die Bahn.

Sofort nun wende dich nach innen:
Das Zentrum findest du da drinnen,
Woran kein Edler zweifeln mag.
Wirst keine Regel da vermissen.
Denn das selbständige Gewissen
Ist Sonne deinem Sittentag.

Den Sinnen hast du dann zu trauen,
Kein Falsches lassen sie dich schauen,
Wenn dein Verstand dich wach erhält.
Mit frischem Blick bemerke freudig
Und wandle, sicher wie geschmeidig,
Durch Auen reichbegabter Welt.

Genieße mäßig Füll und Segen;
Vernunft sei überall zugegen,
Wo Leben sich des Lebens freut.

And so, rise! Brighter and brighter,
on a clear course, in full splendor!
Even if my heart beats painfully faster,
the night is more than full of bliss.

## Legacy

No being can crumble into nothingness!
The Eternal continues to stir within all things;
nourish yourself on Being, and be happy!
Being is eternal: for laws
preserve the living treasures
with which the universe has adorned itself.

The truth was discovered long since,
and has created an alliance of noble minds;
hold on to the old truth!
Son of earth, thank the wise man
who showed it the path by which it circles the sun,
and showed that path to its siblings.

Now immediately turn your thoughts inward:
there you will find the central point
about which no noble-minded man can have doubts.
There you will find no rule missing.
For the independent conscience
plays the role of the sun to your ethical day.

Next, you have to trust your senses;
they do not allow you to observe anything incorrect
if your understanding keeps you alert.
Cheerfully make observations with fresh eyes
and walk, firmly but with suppleness,
through the meadows of a richly endowed world.

Make moderate use of abundance and plenty;
let reason be at hand in every place
where life enjoys life.

Dann ist Vergangenheit beständig,
Das Künftige voraus lebendig,
Der Augenblick ist Ewigkeit.

Und war es endlich dir gelungen,
Und bist du vom Gefühl durchdrungen:
Was fruchtbar ist, allein ist wahr –
Du prüfst das allgemeine Walten,
Es wird nach seiner Weise schalten,
Geselle dich zur kleinsten Schar.

Und wie von alters her, im stillen,
Ein Liebewerk nach eignem Willen
Der Philosoph, der Dichter schuf,
So wirst du schönste Gunst erzielen:
Denn edlen Seelen vorzufühlen
Ist wünschenswertester Beruf.

Then the past will be of permanence,
the future will come to life in advance,
and the present moment will be eternity.

And once you've finally succeeded,
and have been permeated with the feeling
"Only what is productive is true,"
you can probe the doings of society,
which will operate according to its own rules;
associate yourself with the smallest number of people.

And, as of old, the philosopher
and the poet created, in silent seclusion,
a labor of love in pursuance of their own will,
so you, too, will obtain the highest favor:
for to have a presentiment of what noble souls will some day accomplish
is the most desirable function of man.

# Alphabetical List of German Titles

*Only distinct titles assigned by Goethe or later editors are listed here;*
*for poems identified by their first lines, see the Alphabetical List of German*
*First Lines. In accordance with German usage, the definitive article counts*
*within the alphabetization: thus, "Der Fischer," not "Fischer, Der."*
*Alternate titles are included in this list.*

# Alphabetical List of German First Lines

A CATALOG OF SELECTED
# DOVER BOOKS
IN ALL FIELDS OF INTEREST

# A CATALOG OF SELECTED DOVER
# BOOKS IN ALL FIELDS OF INTEREST

CONCERNING THE SPIRITUAL IN ART, Wassily Kandinsky. Pioneering work by father of abstract art. Thoughts on color theory, nature of art. Analysis of earlier masters. 12 illustrations. 80pp. of text. 5⅜ x 8½.                    23411-8 Pa. $4.95

ANIMALS: 1,419 Copyright-Free Illustrations of Mammals, Birds, Fish, Insects, etc., Jim Harter (ed.). Clear wood engravings present, in extremely lifelike poses, over 1,000 species of animals. One of the most extensive pictorial sourcebooks of its kind. Captions. Index. 284pp. 9 x 12.                    23766-4 Pa. $14.95

CELTIC ART: The Methods of Construction, George Bain. Simple geometric techniques for making Celtic interlacements, spirals, Kells-type initials, animals, humans, etc. Over 500 illustrations. 160pp. 9 x 12. (USO)                    22923-8 Pa. $9.95

AN ATLAS OF ANATOMY FOR ARTISTS, Fritz Schider. Most thorough reference work on art anatomy in the world. Hundreds of illustrations, including selections from works by Vesalius, Leonardo, Goya, Ingres, Michelangelo, others. 593 illustrations. 192pp. 7⅛ x 10¼.                    20241-0 Pa. $9.95

CELTIC HAND STROKE-BY-STROKE (Irish Half-Uncial from "The Book of Kells"): An Arthur Baker Calligraphy Manual, Arthur Baker. Complete guide to creating each letter of the alphabet in distinctive Celtic manner. Covers hand position, strokes, pens, inks, paper, more. Illustrated. 48pp. 8¼ x 11.                    24336-2 Pa. $3.95

EASY ORIGAMI, John Montroll. Charming collection of 32 projects (hat, cup, pelican, piano, swan, many more) specially designed for the novice origami hobbyist. Clearly illustrated easy-to-follow instructions insure that even beginning papercrafters will achieve successful results. 48pp. 8¼ x 11.                    27298-2 Pa. $3.50

THE COMPLETE BOOK OF BIRDHOUSE CONSTRUCTION FOR WOODWORKERS, Scott D. Campbell. Detailed instructions, illustrations, tables. Also data on bird habitat and instinct patterns. Bibliography. 3 tables. 63 illustrations in 15 figures. 48pp. 5¼ x 8½.                    24407-5 Pa. $2.50

BLOOMINGDALE'S ILLUSTRATED 1886 CATALOG: Fashions, Dry Goods and Housewares, Bloomingdale Brothers. Famed merchants' extremely rare catalog depicting about 1,700 products: clothing, housewares, firearms, dry goods, jewelry, more. Invaluable for dating, identifying vintage items. Also, copyright-free graphics for artists, designers. Co-published with Henry Ford Museum & Greenfield Village. 160pp. 8¼ x 11.                    25780-0 Pa. $10.95

HISTORIC COSTUME IN PICTURES, Braun & Schneider. Over 1,450 costumed figures in clearly detailed engravings–from dawn of civilization to end of 19th century. Captions. Many folk costumes. 256pp. 8⅜ x 11¾.                    23150-X Pa. $12.95

PERSPECTIVE FOR ARTISTS, Rex Vicat Cole. Depth, perspective of sky and sea, shadows, much more, not usually covered. 391 diagrams, 81 reproductions of drawings and paintings. 279pp. 5⅜ x 8½.                     22487-2 Pa. $7.95

DRAWING THE LIVING FIGURE, Joseph Sheppard. Innovative approach to artistic anatomy focuses on specifics of surface anatomy, rather than muscles and bones. Over 170 drawings of live models in front, back and side views, and in widely varying poses. Accompanying diagrams. 177 illustrations. Introduction. Index. 144pp. 8⅜ x11¼.                     26723-7 Pa. $8.95

GOTHIC AND OLD ENGLISH ALPHABETS: 100 Complete Fonts, Dan X. Solo. Add power, elegance to posters, signs, other graphics with 100 stunning copyright-free alphabets: Blackstone, Dolbey, Germania, 97 more—including many lower-case, numerals, punctuation marks. 104pp. 8⅛ x 11.                     24695-7 Pa. $8.95

HOW TO DO BEADWORK, Mary White. Fundamental book on craft from simple projects to five-bead chains and woven works. 106 illustrations. 142pp. 5⅜ x 8.
                                  20697-1 Pa. $4.95

THE BOOK OF WOOD CARVING, Charles Marshall Sayers. Finest book for beginners discusses fundamentals and offers 34 designs. "Absolutely first rate . . . well thought out and well executed."–E. J. Tangerman. 118pp. 7¾ x 10⅝.
                                  23654-4 Pa. $6.95

ILLUSTRATED CATALOG OF CIVIL WAR MILITARY GOODS: Union Army Weapons, Insignia, Uniform Accessories, and Other Equipment, Schuyler, Hartley, and Graham. Rare, profusely illustrated 1846 catalog includes Union Army uniform and dress regulations, arms and ammunition, coats, insignia, flags, swords, rifles, etc. 226 illustrations. 160pp. 9 x 12.                     24939-5 Pa. $10.95

WOMEN'S FASHIONS OF THE EARLY 1900s: An Unabridged Republication of "New York Fashions, 1909," National Cloak & Suit Co. Rare catalog of mail-order fashions documents women's and children's clothing styles shortly after the turn of the century. Captions offer full descriptions, prices. Invaluable resource for fashion, costume historians. Approximately 725 illustrations. 128pp. 8⅜ x 11¼.
                                  27276-1 Pa. $11.95

THE 1912 AND 1915 GUSTAV STICKLEY FURNITURE CATALOGS, Gustav Stickley. With over 200 detailed illustrations and descriptions, these two catalogs are essential reading and reference materials and identification guides for Stickley furniture. Captions cite materials, dimensions and prices. 112pp. 6½ x 9¼.
                                  26676-1 Pa. $9.95

EARLY AMERICAN LOCOMOTIVES, John H. White, Jr. Finest locomotive engravings from early 19th century: historical (1804–74), main-line (after 1870), special, foreign, etc. 147 plates. 142pp. 11⅜ x 8¼.        22772-3 Pa. $10.95

THE TALL SHIPS OF TODAY IN PHOTOGRAPHS, Frank O. Braynard. Lavishly illustrated tribute to nearly 100 majestic contemporary sailing vessels: Amerigo Vespucci, Clearwater, Constitution, Eagle, Mayflower, Sea Cloud, Victory, many more. Authoritative captions provide statistics, background on each ship. 190 black-and-white photographs and illustrations. Introduction. 128pp. 8⅞ x 11¾.
                                  27163-3 Pa. $14.95

EARLY NINETEENTH-CENTURY CRAFTS AND TRADES, Peter Stockham (ed.). Extremely rare 1807 volume describes to youngsters the crafts and trades of the day: brickmaker, weaver, dressmaker, bookbinder, ropemaker, saddler, many more. Quaint prose, charming illustrations for each craft. 20 black-and-white line illustrations. 192pp. 4⅝ x 6.                                27293-1 Pa. $4.95

VICTORIAN FASHIONS AND COSTUMES FROM HARPER'S BAZAR, 1867–1898, Stella Blum (ed.). Day costumes, evening wear, sports clothes, shoes, hats, other accessories in over 1,000 detailed engravings. 320pp. 9⅜ x 12¼.
22990-4 Pa. $15.95

GUSTAV STICKLEY, THE CRAFTSMAN, Mary Ann Smith. Superb study surveys broad scope of Stickley's achievement, especially in architecture. Design philosophy, rise and fall of the Craftsman empire, descriptions and floor plans for many Craftsman houses, more. 86 black-and-white halftones. 31 line illustrations. Introduction 208pp. 6½ x 9¼.                                27210-9 Pa. $9.95

THE LONG ISLAND RAIL ROAD IN EARLY PHOTOGRAPHS, Ron Ziel. Over 220 rare photos, informative text document origin ( 1844) and development of rail service on Long Island. Vintage views of early trains, locomotives, stations, passengers, crews, much more. Captions. 8⅞ x 11¾.                                26301-0 Pa. $13.95

THE BOOK OF OLD SHIPS: From Egyptian Galleys to Clipper Ships, Henry B. Culver. Superb, authoritative history of sailing vessels, with 80 magnificent line illustrations. Galley, bark, caravel, longship, whaler, many more. Detailed, informative text on each vessel by noted naval historian. Introduction. 256pp. 5⅜ x 8½.
27332-6 Pa. $7.95

TEN BOOKS ON ARCHITECTURE, Vitruvius. The most important book ever written on architecture. Early Roman aesthetics, technology, classical orders, site selection, all other aspects. Morgan translation. 331pp. 5⅜ x 8½.    20645-9 Pa. $8.95

THE HUMAN FIGURE IN MOTION, Eadweard Muybridge. More than 4,500 stopped-action photos, in action series, showing undraped men, women, children jumping, lying down, throwing, sitting, wrestling, carrying, etc. 390pp. 7⅞ x 10⅝.
20204-6 Clothbd. $27.95

TREES OF THE EASTERN AND CENTRAL UNITED STATES AND CANADA, William M. Harlow. Best one-volume guide to 140 trees. Full descriptions, woodlore, range, etc. Over 600 illustrations. Handy size. 288pp. 4½ x 6⅜.
20395-6 Pa. $6.95

SONGS OF WESTERN BIRDS, Dr. Donald J. Borror. Complete song and call repertoire of 60 western species, including flycatchers, juncoes, cactus wrens, many more—includes fully illustrated booklet.        Cassette and manual 99913-0 $8.95

GROWING AND USING HERBS AND SPICES, Milo Miloradovich. Versatile handbook provides all the information needed for cultivation and use of all the herbs and spices available in North America. 4 illustrations. Index. Glossary. 236pp. 5⅜ x 8½.
25058-X Pa. $6.95

BIG BOOK OF MAZES AND LABYRINTHS, Walter Shepherd. 50 mazes and labyrinths in all—classical, solid, ripple, and more—in one great volume. Perfect inexpensive puzzler for clever youngsters. Full solutions. 112pp. 8⅛ x 11.
22951-3 Pa. $4.95

8425

**THE INFLUENCE OF SEA POWER UPON HISTORY, 1660–1783,** A. T. Mahan. Influential classic of naval history and tactics still used as text in war colleges. First paperback edition. 4 maps. 24 battle plans. 640pp. 5⅜ x 8½. 25509-3 Pa. $14.95

**THE STORY OF THE TITANIC AS TOLD BY ITS SURVIVORS,** Jack Winocour (ed.). What it was really like. Panic, despair, shocking inefficiency, and a little heroism. More thrilling than any fictional account. 26 illustrations. 320pp. 5⅜ x 8½. 20610-6 Pa. $8.95

**FAIRY AND FOLK TALES OF THE IRISH PEASANTRY,** William Butler Yeats (ed.). Treasury of 64 tales from the twilight world of Celtic myth and legend: "The Soul Cages," "The Kildare Pooka," "King O'Toole and his Goose," many more. Introduction and Notes by W. B. Yeats. 352pp. 5⅜ x 8½. 26941-8 Pa. $8.95

**BUDDHIST MAHAYANA TEXTS,** E. B. Cowell and Others (eds.). Superb, accurate translations of basic documents in Mahayana Buddhism, highly important in history of religions. The Buddha-karita of Asvaghosha, Larger Sukhavativyuha, more. 448pp. 5⅜ x 8½. 25552-2 Pa. $12.95

**ONE TWO THREE . . . INFINITY: Facts and Speculations of Science,** George Gamow. Great physicist's fascinating, readable overview of contemporary science: number theory, relativity, fourth dimension, entropy, genes, atomic structure, much more. 128 illustrations. Index. 352pp. 5⅜ x 8½. 25664-2 Pa. $8.95

**ENGINEERING IN HISTORY,** Richard Shelton Kirby, et al. Broad, nontechnical survey of history's major technological advances: birth of Greek science, industrial revolution, electricity and applied science, 20th-century automation, much more. 181 illustrations. ". . . excellent . . ."–*Isis.* Bibliography. vii + 530pp. 5⅜ x 8¼. 26412-2 Pa. $14.95

**DALÍ ON MODERN ART: The Cuckolds of Antiquated Modern Art,** Salvador Dalí. Influential painter skewers modern art and its practitioners. Outrageous evaluations of Picasso, Cézanne, Turner, more. 15 renderings of paintings discussed. 44 calligraphic decorations by Dalí. 96pp. 5⅜ x 8½. (USO) 29220-7 Pa. $4.95

**ANTIQUE PLAYING CARDS: A Pictorial History,** Henry René D'Allemagne. Over 900 elaborate, decorative images from rare playing cards (14th–20th centuries): Bacchus, death, dancing dogs, hunting scenes, royal coats of arms, players cheating, much more. 96pp. 9¼ x 12¼. 29265-7 Pa. $12.95

**MAKING FURNITURE MASTERPIECES: 30 Projects with Measured Drawings,** Franklin H. Gottshall. Step-by-step instructions, illustrations for constructing handsome, useful pieces, among them a Sheraton desk, Chippendale chair, Spanish desk, Queen Anne table and a William and Mary dressing mirror. 224pp. 8½ x 11¼. 29338-6 Pa. $13.95

**THE FOSSIL BOOK: A Record of Prehistoric Life,** Patricia V. Rich et al. Profusely illustrated definitive guide covers everything from single-celled organisms and dinosaurs to birds and mammals and the interplay between climate and man. Over 1,500 illustrations. 760pp. 7½ x 10⅛. 29371-8 Pa. $29.95

*Prices subject to change without notice.*